Rulers of
Ancient Egypt

Other books in the
Profiles in History series:

❦   ❦   ❦

❦

Rulers of Ancient Egypt

Profiles · in · History

Don Nardo, *Book Editor*

Bruce Glassman, *Vice President*
Bonnie Szumski, *Publisher*
Helen Cothran, *Managing Editor*

GREENHAVEN PRESS
An imprint of Thomson Gale, a part of The Thomson Corporation

THOMSON

GALE

Detroit • New York • San Francisco • San Diego • New Haven, Conn.
Waterville, Maine • London • Munich

For more information, contact
Greenhaven Press
27500 Drake Rd.
Farmington Hills, MI 48331-3535
Or you can visit our Internet site at http://www.gale.com

LIBRARY OF CONGRESS CATALOGING-IN-PUBLICATION DATA

Rulers of ancient Egypt / Don Nardo, book editor.
    p. cm. — (Profiles in history)
Includes bibliographical references and index.
ISBN 0-7377-1475-1 (lib. : alk. paper)
    1. Egypt—History—to A.D. 640. 2. Pharaohs. 3. Egypt—Kings and rulers.
I. Nardo, Don, 1947– . II. Series.
DT83.R85 2004
932'.009'9—dc21   2002041631

Contents

Chapter 1: Nationalists, Conquerors, and Builders

Kingdom was Thutmose III, who consolidated
Egypt's empire in Syria-Palestine and set an example as a military hero for later Egyptian rulers.

Chapter 2: Akhenaten: The Heretic Pharaoh

pharaoh Akhenaten appears to be physically deformed, and a number of scholars have advanced intriguing theories to explain this mystery.

Chapter 3: Ramesses II and the Battle of Kadesh

Chapter 4: Cleopatra: Egypt's Last Pharaoh

Foreword

Historians and other scholars have often argued about which forces are most influential in driving the engines of history. A favorite theory in past ages was that powerful supernatural forces—the gods and/or fate—were deciding factors in earthly events. Modern theories, by contrast, have tended to emphasize more natural and less mysterious factors. In the nineteenth century, for example, the great Scottish historian Thomas Carlyle stated, "No great man lives in vain. The history of the world is but the biography of great men." This was the kernel of what came to be known as the "great man" theory of history, the idea that from time to time an unusually gifted, influential man or woman emerges and pushes the course of civilization in a new direction. According to Carlyle:

> Universal History, the history of what man has accomplished in this world, is at bottom the History of the Great Men who have worked here. They were the leaders of men, these great ones; the modelers . . . of whatsoever the general mass of men contrived to do or to attain; all things that we see standing accomplished in the world are properly the outer material result. . . . The soul of the whole world's history, it may justly be considered, were the history of these [persons].

In this view, individuals such as Moses, Buddha, Augustus, Christ, Constantine, Elizabeth I, Thomas Jefferson, Frederick Douglass, Franklin Roosevelt, and Nelson

Mandela accomplished deeds or promoted ideas that sooner or later reshaped human societies in large portions of the globe.

The great man thesis, which was widely popular in the late 1800s and early 1900s, has since been eclipsed by other theories of history. Some scholars accept the "situational" theory. It holds that human leaders and innovators only react to social situations and movements that develop substantially on their own, through random interactions. In this view, Moses achieved fame less because of his unique personal qualities and more because he wisely dealt with the already existing situation of the Hebrews wandering in the desert in search of a new home.

More widely held, however, is a view that in a sense combines the great man and situational theories. Here, major historical periods and political, social, and cultural movements occur when a group of gifted, influential, and like-minded individuals respond to a situation or need over the course of time. In this scenario, Moses is seen as one of a group of prophets who over the course of centuries established important traditions of monotheism; and over time a handful of ambitious, talented pharaohs led ancient Egypt from its emergence as the world's first nation to its great age of conquest and empire. Likewise, the Greek playwrights Sophocles and Euripides, the Elizabethan playwright Shakespeare, and the American playwright Eugene O'Neill all advanced the art of drama, leading it to its present form.

The books in the Profiles in History series chronicle and examine in detail the leading figures in some of history's most important historical periods and movements. Some, like those covering Egypt's leading pharaohs and the most influential U.S. presidents, deal with national leaders guiding a great people through good times and bad. Other volumes in the series examine the leaders of important, constructive social movements, such as those that sought to abolish slavery in the nineteenth century and fought for human rights in the twentieth century. And some, such as the one on Hitler and his henchmen, profile far less constructive, though no less historically important, groups of leaders.

Each book in the series begins with a detailed essay providing crucial background information on the historical period or movement being covered. The main body of the volume consists of a series of shorter essays, each covering an important individual in that period or movement. Where appropriate, two or more essays are devoted to a particularly influential person. Some of the essays provide biographical information; while others, including primary sources by or about the person, focus in on his or her specific deeds, ideas, speeches, or followers. More primary source documents, providing further detail, appear in an appendix, followed by a thorough, up-to-date bibliography that guides interested readers to further research. Overall, the volumes of the Profiles in History series offer a balanced view of the march of civilization by demonstrating how certain individuals make history and at the same time are products of the deeds and movements of their predecessors.

Introduction: Egypt Under the Pharaohs

$\mathbf{A}$ncient Egypt was governed by pharaohs for a period of a little more than three thousand years. The term "pharaoh" is an ancient Greek version of the even more ancient Egyptian *per-aa*, meaning "great house." It originally referred to the royal palace and was not used by the Egyptians themselves to describe their kings until the era of the New Kingdom, which began about 1550 B.C. But for the sake of convenience, modern studies of ancient Egypt use the term pharaoh to describe all Egyptian kings beginning with the one who forged the Egyptian nation some fifteen centuries before the advent of the famous New Kingdom.

How the Nation-State and Pharaoh Came to Be

This achievement was monumental because it marked the first known appearance of a centralized nation-state in world history. To understand its significance at the time, one must first consider what Egypt was like before the advent of the pharaohs. The region had long been inhabited by hunter-gatherers who had subsisted in the Nile River valley for at least a hundred thousand years (and probably considerably longer). Over time, migrants from Palestine, Lybia (west of Egypt), and Nubia (south of Egypt) entered the area. And slowly, small-scale farming began in the Nile's marshlands. Farming had become the chief means of livelihood in the whole Nile valley by the early years of Egypt's Predynastic period (ca. 5500–3100 B.C.). Finally, large-scale farming that took advantage of the Nile's yearly floods was in place by about 4000 B.C. or somewhat later.

The large, dependable food source provided by agriculture and the settled way of life that was needed to accomplish it was the first major step toward a centralized population, cities to house it, and the establishment of kingdoms with cultural identities. Large-scale cooperative efforts of farmers and villagers stimulated rapid and significant developments in social organization and the production of new tools, utensils, stone vessels (and eventually pottery ones), and other artifacts. During the fourth millennium B.C., two distinct kingdoms evolved, one in the south (called Upper Egypt because it lay closer to the Nile's source), the other in the north (Lower Egypt). Each realm had a recognized kinglike leader, about whom virtually nothing is known.

It was probably inevitable that these kingdoms and their rulers would become rivals and engage in wars. And sooner or later one was bound to decisively defeat the other. The result was that Upper and Lower Egypt came together into a single nation-state around 3100 B.C., an achievement credited to a ruler named Menes (or Narmer). As the first king of Egypt's first dynasty (family line of rulers), he was later recognized as the country's first pharaoh. To emphasize the importance of national unity, Menes founded a new capital city, Memphis, at the boundary between the former rival kingdoms. He also adopted a crown that combined the main features of the crowns worn by the leaders of those kingdoms.

Of prime importance to the subsequent development of Egyptian society, Menes and his immediate successors established themselves as absolute monarchs whose word was law. Moreover, they further cemented their authority by assuming divine attributes; they were not merely kings, but god-kings, earthly manifestations of the mystical deities thought to have created the world. After that, with few exceptions, the vast social and economic gap between the royal family (and other high-born nobles) and the common people was firmly established. And the average Egyptian knew and accepted his or her humble place in a greater universal scheme overseen by the pharaoh. Indeed, "the king rose to become the overpowering focus of earthly life in reality as well as in the arts," commented the late and noted scholar Chester G. Starr.

> [In sculptures and paintings, the pharaoh] is overwhelming in size as he strikes down his enemies. Writing was largely used to celebrate his deeds. . . . [He] governed all aspects of life with the aid of a simple central administration, directed by a vizier and largely composed of his sons and other relatives. Below him, nomarchs [each the head of a local district called a nome] moved from nome to nome to conduct the local administration. . . . The monarch . . . lived and died in great pomp and luxury. About his tomb stretched hundreds and thousands of graves of his attendants and officials. . . . The ruler also had great responsibilities, which explains the willingness of his people to heap up the pyramids [built as tombs for the pharaohs]. He was a god on earth, who assured the rise of the Nile, the prosperity of the land, and its peace and order. . . . To unify itself, in sum, early Egypt took the intellectually simple approach of raising its ruler to the position of a superhuman symbol . . . in human form.[1]

This lofty position of divine father figure for the nation was only part of a dual role the pharaoh played. He was also the supreme commander of the country's armies and was expected to lead those armies in battle. At first, such battles were not very common, mainly because during the Old Kingdom and Middle Kingdom (encompassing the first sixteen hundred years of the nation's existence) the pharaohs saw no urgent need to conquer other nations. Largely shaping this outlook was Egypt's unique geographical situation. Its population was concentrated in the narrow, fertile ribbon of land running along the Nile's banks, and for a long time Egypt remained more or less isolated from the outside world by vast expanses of arid desert. Over time this brought about a rather distorted sense of self-importance, as the Egyptians came to believe that they lay at the center of things and that everything else in the universe revolved around them and their culture.

In this view, foreigners were secondary beings, generally hostile, backward, evil, and/or cowardly individuals who posed a potential threat to the cosmic order. This Egyptian air of superiority is evident in a twenty-second-century B.C. kernel of advice from an Egyptian ruler to his son:

> [Behold] the miserable Asiatic; he is wretched because of the [inferior] place he is [inhabiting]. Short of water, bare of wood, its paths are many and painful because of mountains. He does not dwell in one place, [but instead] food propels his legs [i.e., he lives a nomadic existence, seen as inferior to the settled agricultural life along the Nile].[2]

Foreigners, then, were little more than lowly pests dwelling beyond and occasionally threatening Egypt's borders. So any military operation an early Egyptian pharaoh launched was seen as a sort of police action or punishment; and the principal goal was to restore the natural order that the foreigners had temporarily upset.

Thus, for a long time Egyptian rulers did not seriously consider the idea of conquering peoples and lands located beyond Egypt's immediate vicinity. Some Old and Middle Kingdom pharaohs did send troops into Nubia and other nearby areas. But these expeditions were not efforts to create an empire. Rather, they consisted of raids to gather valuable natural resources, punitive measures against rebels, and above all restorations of the safety of the country's borders. The very integrity of the Egyptian nation seemed to depend on the safety of the borders because these barriers were all that separated its civilized little world from the dark, chaotic forces perceived as lurking outside.

Beginning of the New Kingdom

Eventually, however, this outlook changed. Egypt finally expanded its interests beyond its borders and acquired an empire, a policy that at first was largely a response to what the Egyptians saw as one of their country's greatest humiliations. In about 1650 B.C. a group of immigrants who had recently established themselves as workers and soldiers in Egypt rose up and took over the northern section of the country by force. (The pharaohs managed to maintain a power base in the south, with their capital at Thebes.) The ascendancy of these interlopers—the Hyksos—marked the end of the Middle Kingdom and beginning of the Second Intermediate Period (ca. 1650–ca. 1550 B.C.). The worst nightmare Egyptian leaders could imagine—an intrusion of "barbarians" from beyond the borders— had become a terrifying and humiliating reality.

The Egyptians managed to drive the hated Hyksos out of Egypt by the mid–sixteenth century B.C., initiating the period modern scholars call the New Kingdom (ca. 1550–1069 B.C.). But the century-long occupation of the country had left its people scarred and their outlook on life and the world forever changed. First, there was a major upsurge in nationalism and patriotism during and immediately following the expulsion of the

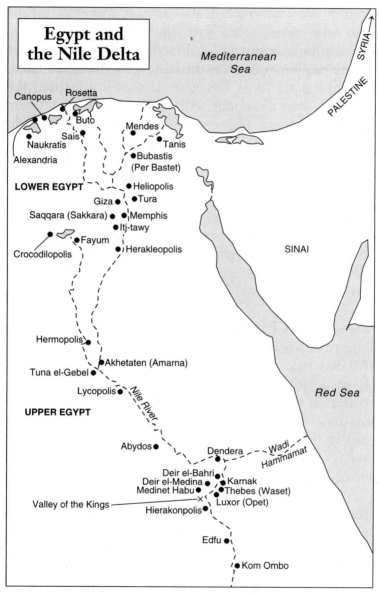

Egypt and the Nile Delta

Mediterranean Sea

SYRIA →

PALESTINE

Canopus   Rosetta
Buto
Mendes
Sais   Tanis
Naukratis
Bubastis
Alexandria   (Per Bastet)

LOWER EGYPT   Heliopolis
Giza   Tura
Saqqara (Sakkara)   Memphis
Itj-tawy
Fayum
Crocodilopolis   Herakleopolis

SINAI

Hermopolis
Akhetaten (Amarna)
Tuna el-Gebel
Lycopolis   Nile River

UPPER EGYPT

Red Sea

Abydos   Dendera   Wadi Hammamat
Deir el-Bahri
Deir el-Medina   Karnak
Medinet Habu   Thebes (Waset)
Valley of the Kings   Luxor (Opet)
Hierakonpolis

Edfu

Kom Ombo

Hyksos. Kamose, last pharaoh of the Seventeenth Dynasty, and Ahmose, first ruler of the Eighteenth, waged several campaigns as part of a war of national liberation; they and their followers directed their wrath not only against the Hyksos, but also against those Egyptians who had collaborated with the occupiers. Thus, by eliminating competing local factions the conflict had a strong unifying effect on the nation and its inhabitants. At the same time, Egyptian leaders had learned the hard way that the country's borders were not and may never again be totally secure. Therefore they had to do more than simply guard the borders; they must launch preemptive strikes. This entailed going past these artificial barriers and confronting any enemies that posed a potential threat, in the process expanding Egypt's sphere of influence into neighboring lands. As a result, Egypt became a major military state, and imperialism, one nation's attempted military and/or political domination of others, became a defining feature of the government of the New Kingdom.

The Age of Empire

The final liberation of the country from Hyksos control occurred under Ahmose. After driving north from Thebes, he laid siege to the main Hyksos stronghold of Avaris (in the eastern section of the Nile Delta), then drove the intruders into Palestine. Worried that the enemy might try to regroup and launch a counteroffensive, the pharaoh pursued the remaining Hyksos and killed or captured most of them.

In this warlike endeavor, Ahmose set a precedent; practically every succeeding New Kingdom pharaoh was eager to push beyond the borders, as well as to prove his military capabilities and godlike courage. This not only made the country safer, but also greatly enhanced the king's official image as portrayed in royal decrees, building inscriptions, paintings, and other modes of propaganda. Waging and winning wars was clearly an effective way of elevating his image. As an invincible war hero and national savior, he could be confident of keeping the allegiance of his people. To maintain this superhuman image, almost all of Ahmose's successors led one or more military expeditions into Syria-Palestine or Nubia or both. One such campaign—a thrust into Nubia by Thutmose I (reigned 1504–1492 B.C.)—was celebrated in an inscription found at Tombos (near the Nile's third cataract):

> He has overthrown the chief of the Nubians; the black man is helpless, defenseless in his grasp. . . . The Nubian troglodytes [primitive cave dwellers, a standard insult rather than literal description] fall by the sword, and are thrust aside in their lands; their foulness . . . floods their valleys.[3]

Larger and more crucial were the campaigns of Thutmose III, who reigned from 1479 to 1425 B.C. He is sometimes referred to as the "Egyptian Alexander the Great," after the famous ancient Greek conqueror, or the "Napoléon of Egypt," after the equally famous modern French conqueror. Under Thutmose, Egypt's empire (which might be more accurately described as a sphere of influence, since the pharaohs controlled conquered lands through local puppet rulers) expanded to its largest extent—about four hundred thousand square miles, almost twice the size of the state of Texas.

This was an impressive feat considering that other great Near Eastern powers had designs on Syria-Palestine, the centerpiece of Egypt's sphere of influence. In the early years of Thutmose's reign, the powerful kingdom of Mitanni, situated northeast of Syria, had managed to impose its own will on many of the small states in the region. To put down this "rebellion" against Egyptian authority, in 1457 B.C. the pharaoh marched northeast with a large army. He discovered that the enemy army was using the city of Megiddo (the biblical Armageddon) as its base and decided to launch an attack. The daring Thutmose led his troops through a narrow, dangerous mountain pass and surprised the enemy on the plain near the city. According to Thutmose's official annals, the pharaoh led a frontal assault at dawn:

> Early in the morning, behold, command was given to the entire army to move. His majesty went forth in a chariot of electrum [an alloy of gold and silver], arrayed in his weapons of war, like [the god] Horus, the Smiter, lord of power. . . . The southern wing of this army of his majesty was at the northwest of Megiddo while his majesty was in their center. . . . Then his majesty prevailed against them at the head of his army. The fear of his majesty had entered [their hearts], their arms were powerless, [and] his serpent diadem [crown] was victorious among them. Then were captured their horses, their chariots of gold and silver . . . [and] their champions lay stretched out like fishes on the ground.[4]

Fruitful Builders and an Infamous Revolutionary

Thutmose followed up his victory by carrying back to Egypt the sons of some thirty-six local rulers and holding them hostage; this ensured that their fathers would remain loyal to Egypt rather than Mitanni. Over the course of years, these young men were indoctrinated with Egyptian ideas and customs and sent back to their home cities to become puppet rulers friendly to Egypt.

Meanwhile, not all of the activities of Egypt's New Kingdom rulers were war related. Some, like their Old Kingdom predecessors who had erected the pyramids, were fruitful, even great builders. One of the more accomplished was a strong queen, Hatshepsut, daughter of Thutmose I. From 1473 to 1458 B.C., she was regent to and then coruler with her stepson, the future conqueror Thutmose III. Among her achievements was the rebuilding of temples and other structures ruined by the Hyksos, as she boasted in this temple inscription:

Hear you, all persons! You people as many as you are! I have done this according to the design of my heart. . . . I have restored that which was ruins, I have raised up that which was unfinished since the Asiatics [the Hyksos] were in the midst of Avaris of the Northland, and the barbarians were in the midst of them, overthrowing that which was made, while they ruled in ignorance of [i.e., did not recognize] Ra [the Egyptian sun god].[5]

Another pharaoh who was more interested in internal affairs than military conquests was Amenhotep IV (reigned 1352–1336 B.C.). He became famous (in his own time "infamous" is perhaps a more accurate term) for launching a religious revolution that sought to impose sudden and massive changes in a society that was by nature highly traditional and slow to adopt new ideas. Rejecting the accepted gods, he singled out one— Aten, the face of the sun—for worship, changed his name to Akhenaten ("servant of Aten"), and built a new capital city, naming it Ahketaten. Noted scholar Charles Freeman sums up the "maverick" pharaoh's accomplishments, mistakes, and ultimate fate:

Akhenaten's motives for this religious revolution are not clear. . . . He may simply have been trying to assert his own independence from the power of the temples, or [may] genuinely have developed his own religious beliefs. Whatever his motives, he had set himself a massive task. Religious belief was so deeply imbedded in the Egyptian world picture that Akhenaten was, in effect, challenging the intellectual structure of the state. The impact was profound. Many temples were closed down and their goods were confiscated. The economic structure of the state was upset as lands were transferred directly to the king. . . . Five years after his accession Akhenaten moved his capital downriver to a virgin site. . . . The move presumably reflected the king's desire to break free completely from the weight of Egyptian tradition. . . .

[But] the new religion did not catch on. . . . To replace [the traditional gods] by a single physical entity
. . . was a cultural shock far greater than the Egyptians could absorb. Even the workmen building [the
new capital] stayed loyal to their traditional gods. . . .
When Akhenaten died in about 1336 B.C. (of unknown causes) the country was left in some confusion. . . . It is hardly surprising that it was a general,
Horemheb, who eventually succeeded [to the throne
and restored the old gods]. He even extended his
reign backwards so as to delete that of Akhenaten
[whose name was erased from most monuments].[6]

A New Series of Warrior Pharaohs

Horemheb did much more than reverse Akhenaten's
ill-fated revolution. The new pharaoh proved himself a
prodigious builder, overseeing fresh construction projects at the growing temple complexes at Luxor and
Karnak. Horemheb also took up the imperial sword
that Akhenaten had temporarily dropped, launching
campaigns into both Syria-Palestine and Nubia. It was
necessary to refocus the nation's attention on foreign
and military affairs, for the fourteenth century B.C. wit-
nessed the emergence of a much greater threat to
Egypt that Mitanni had ever been. A generation after
Thutmose III had fought Mitanni, Thutmose IV had
made peace with the enemy; and after that Mitanni was
never again a serious threat to Egypt. However, at that
same moment far to the north, in the heart of Asia Minor (what is now Turkey), a new, very formidable empire was rising ominously—Hatti, land of the Hittites.

The aggressive Hittites moved south into Syria and
southeast into Mitanni. The latter, pressed by the Meso-
potamian kingdom of Assyria on one side and the Hittites on the other, buckled under the strain. Eventually,
the Hittite king Suppiluliumas I drove into Mitanni's
heartland and sacked its capital of Washukkanni, after

which the small states and walled cities of Syria, including Aleppo, Ugarit, Carchemish, and Kadesh, fell to the Hittites one after another.

The first of a new series of warrior pharaohs, Horemheb recognized the growing Hittite threat, although he never actually met the new enemy in battle. When he failed to produce a male heir, he passed the throne to one of his generals, Ramesses, who, as the pharaoh Ramesses I, founded the Nineteenth Dynasty. Ramesses' son and successor, Seti I, turned out to be the first pharaoh to actually fight the Hittites. About 1290 B.C., Seti led an army north and defeated the Hittites near Kadesh, his scribes later recording in an inscription on a relief at Karnak: "His majesty made a great slaughter, smiting the Asiatics, beating down the Hittites, slaying their chiefs . . . charging among them like a tongue of fire!"[7] However, the Hittites were both resourceful and persistent and they soon regained control over much of Syria. This set the scene for a major confrontation between Seti's son, Ramesses II, and Hatti's new king, Muwatallis.

When the second Ramesses assumed the throne in 1279 B.C., he was in his twenties and filled with vigor and ambition. He wished to follow up on Seti's campaign and restore all of Syria to the huge sphere of influence the early New Kingdom pharaohs had maintained in the region. With this goal in mind, in the summer of the fourth year of his reign (ca. 1275 B.C.), he set out with an army, forged his way northward through Palestine, and captured the Syrian region of Amurru, lying to the southwest of the walled town of Kadesh. Eventually Ramesses reached Kadesh, where Muwatallis had laid a trap for him by hiding most of the Hittite army beyond the town. A large corps of Hittite chariots attacked and decimated an Egyptian regiment and only some quick thinking and a bold counterattack by Ramesses saved his own army from total defeat. In the customary post-battle propaganda, the pharaoh claimed a great victory; but in truth the engagement was indecisive. Soon afterward Ramesses and Muwatallis reluctantly agreed to a temporary peace. And a few years later Ramesses signed a peace treaty with a new Hittite king, Hattusilis III.

The Pharaohs and the Nation in Decline

In the years that followed, the Hittite menace receded, but new threats to Egypt's stability materialized. Unfortunately, however, with the exception of a twentieth-dynasty pharaoh—Ramesses III—Egypt no longer had a string of strong warrior pharaohs to inspire the armies and maintain the far-flung empire. The biggest challenge came in the thirteenth and twelfth centuries B.C., when Egypt came under direct assault from the northwest and north by groups of foreigners the Egyptians collectively called the "Sea Peoples." The invaders came in waves, each apparently larger and more threatening than the one before it. In the fifth year of the reign of the pharaoh Merneptah (about 1208 B.C.), a force of Sea Peoples invaded Egypt from the northwest. Fortunately for Egypt, Merneptah managed to defeat them in a pitched battle near the western side of the delta.

The five pharaohs who followed Merneptah heard ominous reports of devastation caused by new waves of Sea Peoples in Syria and other Near Eastern lands. Then, in the eighth year of Ramesses III's reign (ca. 1174 B.C.), the largest wave of Sea Peoples yet bore down on northern Egypt. Somewhere in the Nile Delta, Ramesses rallied his forces and defeated the attackers in a naval battle, a victory the pharaoh captured for the ages in a magnificent stone relief in his mortuary temple.

However, this moment of triumph turned out to be the last major victory the Egyptian military ever enjoyed and a turning point in the country's ability to maintain significant influence beyond its own borders. Some of the surviving Sea Peoples settled in Palestine, the last remnant of Egypt's once considerable Asiatic empire. Soon these settlers took control of the region, shutting the Egyptians out. And by the reign of the last New Kingdom pharaoh, Ramesses XI (reigned 1099–1069 B.C.), Egyptian ships were no longer able to collect supplies of cedar wood and other products from the area. Egypt's once formidable military and political power had passed its prime; and in succeeding centuries the decline continued.

During the two historical eras that followed the New Kingdom—the Third Intermediate Period (1069–747 B.C.) and Late Period (747–332 B.C.)—Egypt was wracked by internal dissention and steadily became a second-rate, even a third-rate power. This increasingly left the country vulnerable to attack by foreign empires. Throughout the Third Intermediate Period, two major power bases—one in the Nile Delta, the other in Thebes —each claimed to have the legitimate pharaoh. And at

Egypt During the New Kingdom

Syria

Cyprus

Lebanon

Mediterranean Sea

Palestine

Jerusalem

Rosetta
Alexandria • *Nile Delta*

Dead Sea

Memphis •
Sahara

Sinai Peninsula

Arabia

• Akhetaten

Eastern Desert

Red Sea

Valley of the Kings X • Thebes

Nile River

Abu Simbel •

Nubia

Kush

various times individual cities asserted local independence and power. The military was similarly fragmented, with local princes commanding their own small armies, which sometimes fought one another. Then, at the start of the Late Period (747 B.C.), a dynasty of Nubian kings pushed their way north and took control of much of Lower Egypt. Like their immediate predecessors, they were unable to reunify the country and restore it to its former greatness.

The Assyrian Empire was the first of a series of large foreign powers to overrun and occupy the now seriously weakened Egypt. In 674 B.C., Assyria's King Esarhaddon swept into the Nile valley and subdued most of the countryside around Memphis in less than a month. "Without cessation I slew multitudes of his men," Esarhaddon later said about the Egyptian king, Taharqo.

> Memphis, his royal city, in half a day, with mines, tunnels, assaults, I besieged, I captured . . . I burned with fire. His queen, his harem, his . . . sons and daughters, his property and his goods, his horses, his cattle, his sheep, in countless numbers, I carried off to Assyria.[8]

To their credit, the Egyptians launched a number of rebellions against the Assyrians. But Egyptian leaders no longer had the resources to maintain and train large armies, so they increasingly turned to hiring foreign mercenaries. In particular, they hired Greeks, mostly from western Asia Minor. And this marked the beginning of Egypt's political dealings with and eventual absorption into the classical Greco-Roman world.

Relying on Greek mercenaries, who were superb fighters, the Egyptians tried to maintain their independence from greater powers that rose and fell around them. But these efforts were in vain. In the late sixth century B.C., the Persian Empire, which had absorbed the old Assyrian realm, conquered both Egypt and its main source of military recruits, the Greek cities of Asia Minor. Persian rule was so unpopular in Egypt that when Alexander III (later called "the Great"), a Macedonian-Greek king, entered the country in 332 B.C. as part of his conquest of Persia, he was welcomed as a liberator. This was an illusion, however. Alexander soon died and one of his leading generals, Ptolemy, took control of Egypt and established a Greek dynasty—the Ptolemaic (332–30 B.C.).

Under the Ptolemies, Egypt became part of the greater Greek world that now encompassed the entire eastern Mediterranean sphere. To defend against other Greek kingdoms, the government maintained a strong military. But as time went on, Ptolemaic Egypt became militarily and politically impotent in the face of Rome's rise to dominance over the entire Mediterranean world.

It was into this Roman-dominated Mediterranean world that the last of the Ptolemies, as well as the last independent Egyptian pharaoh, was born. Cleopatra VII, daughter of Ptolemy XII, was a highly intelligent, talented, and ambitious individual, a ruler of the caliber of Hatshepsut, Thutmose III, and Ramesses II; and had Rome not been so strong, she might have reasserted Egypt's former greatness. However, she made the mistake of supporting the wrong side in a crucial civil war that rocked the Roman world in the latter years of her reign. Allying herself with a powerful Roman, Mark Antony, she opposed his rival, Octavian, who defeated them in a large naval battle at Actium, in Greece, in 31 B.C. The following year Cleopatra and Antony committed suicide.

Egypt then became a province of Rome, a prize to be exploited by Octavian, who soon took the title of Augustus, "the revered one," and launched the Roman Empire. In Alexandria, Memphis, Thebes, and other Egyptian cities, there was much disappointment, bitterness, confusion, and despair. Egypt of the pharaohs, whose proud royal traditions stretched back for more than three millennia to Menes' creation of the world's first nation, had faded forever into the realm of past history.

Notes

1. Chester G. Starr, *A History of the Ancient World.* New York: Oxford University Press, 1991, pp. 59–60.

2. Quoted in Miriam Lichtheim, ed., *Ancient Egyptian Literature: A Book of Readings.* 2 vols. Berkeley: University of California Press, 1975–1976, vol. 1, pp. 103–104.

3. Quoted in J.H. Breasted, ed., *Ancient Records of Egypt.* 5 vols. New York: Russell and Russell, 1962, vol. 2, p. 30.

4. Quoted in Breasted, *Ancient Records,* vol. 2, pp. 184–85.

5. Quoted in Breasted, *Ancient Records,* vol. 2, pp. 125–26.

6. Charles Freeman, *Egypt, Greece, and Rome: Civilizations of the Ancient Mediterranean.* New York: Oxford University Press, 1996, pp. 39–42.

7. Quoted in Breasted, *Ancient Records,* vol. 3, p. 72.

8. Quoted in Daniel D. Luckenbill, ed., *Ancient Records of Assyria and Babylonia.* 2 vols. Chicago: University of Chicago Press, 1926. Reprint: New York: Greenwood Press, 1968, vol. 2, p. 227.

Profiles · in · History

Nationalists, Conquerors, and Builders

The First Pharaoh Unifies Egypt

H.W.F. Saggs

This informative discussion of the foundation of ancient Egyptian kingship is by University of Wales scholar H.W.F. Saggs. He first suggests that the divine position of pharaoh grew out of prehistoric ceremonies involving magic and goes on to explain how Menes, the first pharaoh, unified the country, which at the time was divided into two rival kingdoms. The result was the world's first large nation-state. Saggs then discusses the administrative-political system that Menes and his immediate successors put into place, establishing precedents for the many Egyptian rulers and high officials who would govern the country for dozens of centuries.

🐝 🐝 🐝

The crucial political change in early Egypt came at about 3100 or 3000 B.C.; different scholars use different chronologies. Then, according to tradition, Menes, the king of Upper Egypt, conquered Lower Egypt and made the two kingdoms into one. But history shows that a stable major state does not come about suddenly

H.W.F. Saggs, *Civilization Before Greece and Rome*. New Haven, CT: Yale University Press, 1989. Copyright © 1989 by H.W.F. Saggs. Reproduced by permission of the publisher.

as the result of a single incident of conquest. The innovation which we call the unification of Egypt must have been the final stage of a long period of convergence. Yet even if not as sudden as tradition represents it, it did mark a major step in deliberate social organization; by it, Menes made all Egypt into a single political and economic unit—a good half millennium before any comparable development in Mesopotamia. Admittedly there were those in ancient Egypt who might have denied that Menes made the whole into one kingdom, since to the end the Pharaohs preserved the pretence of the duality of the system, not only in their title 'King of Upper and Lower Egypt', but also in wearing a composite crown which incorporated separate crowns for the original two kingdoms; but in practical terms the country was undoubtedly one. To emphasize the essential unity, Menes created a new capital, Memphis, at the point where the two former kingdoms met. Tradition, recorded by [the fifth century B.C. Greek historian] Herodotus but not otherwise proved, recounts that Menes built a dyke to change the course of the Nile, and founded Memphis on the land so reclaimed. Even if this tradition was not literally true, it at least implied a very early explicit recognition that life in Egypt depended upon regulation of the flood waters. . . .

The Aura of a Divine Being

Rule by one man depends upon the existence of sanctions so powerful that the rest of the population are willing to accept his direction unquestioningly. In ancient Egypt the sanctions were religious and had prehistoric origins. In many primitive societies, the central figure is a magician who is believed to be so intimately linked with the supernatural world that he can control rain or fertility and other aspects of life. So long as his magic proves effective, his power is absolute, but when his powers fail he is sent back to the supernatural world by being put to death. The ancient collection of rituals and myths called the Pyramid Texts, from about 2400 B.C. in their extant form but incorporating beliefs from prehistoric times, shows behind the Egyptian king of historical times a magician of this category. That this person was originally put to death when his powers failed is hinted at by traces of cannibalism and human sacrifice in the Pyramid Texts, but the clearest indication is in a ceremony called the Sed festival. This was a ceremony to rejuvenate the king's failing powers after thirty years of rule. It began with the ritual burial of the king, which surely indicates that originally, when the powers of the king or his magician predecessor failed, he was put to death and there was a real burial.

From the beginning, these prehistoric antecedents invested the living king in Egypt with the aura of a divine being. Because the king was an incarnate god, with Egypt's welfare in his care, it was in everyone's interest to conform to his will. His religious sanction was everywhere evident, for he was nominally the chief priest in every temple. The very circumstances of the unification of Egypt may have served to reinforce belief in the divine nature of the pharaoh. If Menes did indeed divert the sacred life-giving Nile and drain a huge area to build a great capital where formerly there had been swamps, his divine powers could not be doubted. Also, since he controlled the whole Nile valley, he unquestionably had power over the water-supply to every part of the land, an aspect of royalty graphically illustrated in one of the earliest representations of a pharaoh, which shows him cutting the dyke of an irrigation canal with a hoe. From very early times the king of united Egypt had measurements taken of the height of the Nile as it was rising in the south, so that he could accurately predict the area which could be irrigated further north. All these factors meant that, from the point of view of an ancient Egyptian, the king was, quite literally, a fertility giver and controller of the Nile and all the life of the land; from the Egyptians' point of view he was, without question, a god upon whom the life of the land depended. Moreover, because of the ease of navigation from one end of the country to the other by means of the gentle Nile, it was relatively easy to produce a unified system of government (even if administered in duplicate for north and south separately). We shall see that the situation was markedly different in south Mesopotamia.

The definiteness of the tradition makes it likely that Menes was a real king, but which? The name does not occur in native Egyptian records. Three kings, known to egyptologists as Scorpion, Narmer, and Hor-aha, have left monuments from about the time attributed to Menes. If one of these kings has to be picked as Menes, the most probable seems to be Narmer, but quite possibly more than one of them contributed to the tradition. This would accord with the probability that the unification was not an innovation abruptly introduced after conquest, but came about gradually over several reigns.

With Menes we enter the Dynastic Period. This terminology derives from an Egyptian priest, Manetho, who at about 300 B.C. compiled in Greek a list of all Egyptian kings from the beginning, divided into thirty dynasties (later extended to thirty-one), with, of course, Menes as the first king of the First Dynasty. Apart from the name and length of reigns of each ruler, Manetho gives us little snippets of information, such as that Menes 'was taken by a hippopotamus and died', or that his successor 'built the palace at Memphis; his writings on anatomy remain, for he was a doctor', or of the third in succession to him that in his time 'a severe famine gripped Egypt'. Particularly notable, from the records of the Third Dynasty ruler Zoser, is the mention of 'Imuthes, regarded by the Egyptians as Asclepios [the Greek god of healing] for his skill in medicine, the inventer of building in hewn stone'; this was the celebrated Imhotep, architect of the Step Pyramid.

The Pharaoh's Advisers and Administrators

There are more theories than evidence about the running of the early Egyptian state. There are virtually no administrative records. . . . [But] there is one type of evidence which is plentiful in this area: the titles of officials. Some scholars have used these in an attempt to build up a picture of the administrative network. Ancient Egyptians who could afford it delighted in arranging for their autobiographies to be written on their tombs, and [noted scholar] Klaus Baer has analysed tomb inscriptions of over 600 notables, who between them recorded nearly 2000 titles in use during the Old Kingdom. But in fact this mass of titles—legal, scribal, fiscal, religious, organizational, linked to the king or the royal court, or purely honorific—tells us less about the details of the administrative system than we might expect. Some titles which obviously began as marks of function quickly became at first markers of rank within a hierarchy and then merely honorific. The excessive number of titles borne by some officials points this up: when we find, as we do, that a particular notable had a string of well over 200 titles, we can be certain that, unless the man was an administrative genius, only a small portion of these can have related to functions he personally performed or carried responsibility for during his working life.

Baer was unable to make any significant links between the 2000 titles and the pattern of administration, but he did show that a large number of the titles could be placed in ranking order, in a way strangely similar to

the British Order of Precedence. What this mass of titles gives us, therefore, is not an outline of the administrative system but a picture of a society obsessed with
considerations of rank. Paradoxically, this nonfunc-
tional use of titles performed a useful function. An
evolving society creates new offices and ceases to need
old ones. But without a mechanism for sweeping away
obsolete offices, there grows up an enormous amount
of unproductive dead wood. Conversion of old func-
tional offices, no longer required, into honorific titles
discharged this burden.

Although official titles do not give us an adequate
picture of how the early Egyptian state was run, the
material does enable us to extract information about a
few of the greatest offices in the state, sufficient to give
us a rough sketch of the administrative framework,
mainly in the time of the Fifth Dynasty. At that period
all senior functions in the state were shared amongst six
classes of official; these bore the titles, the Overseer of
the Great Mansions, the Overseer of the Scribes of the
Royal Records, the Overseer of Works, the Overseer of
Granaries, the Overseer of the Treasuries, and what we
usually translate as the Vizier.

The 'Great Mansions' of the first title were the courts
of justice. There are indications that there were originally six such courts, but their location is unknown.

The Overseer of the Scribes of the Royal Records
was the head of the scribal administration, responsible
for the preparation and filing of all state documents.
There was at least one occasion during the Fifth Dynasty when two persons held this title simultaneously;
since one of the two was the vizier, the greatest officer
of state, he presumably had overall control, leaving the
other holder of the title to supervise details.

The Overseer of Works was responsible for organiz-
ing work-forces for such operations as building, agri-

culture, expeditions to distant places to obtain materials, and probably (although there is no specific Old Kingdom evidence) digging and maintaining canals. Several holders may have shared this title, each responsible for a particular sector of public works.

The general area of the duties of the Overseer of the Granaries is obvious, but the details are not clear. Sometimes there were simultaneous holders of the title. Little is known of the location of state granaries, but these officials presumably used them to stockpile corn against future shortages as Joseph is said to have done in Genesis 41:48–9; since the state could not survive unless it kept its peasantry fed, this was a vital need. There were also granaries on private estates, where the Overseers of Granaries may have been responsible for assessment for taxation. This would explain their close connection with the Overseer of the Treasuries. . . .

The most important officer in the state administrative system was undoubtedly the vizier. His office must already have existed by the beginning of the Third Dynasty, since the title occurs on stone vessels found beneath the Step Pyramid, built by the first king of that Dynasty. The earliest viziers were all royal princes, a relic from the original situation in which the king kept all authority within the circle of his kinsmen. The people nearest to the pharaoh in life were also those nearest in death, and the grouping of tombs associated with pyramids in Saqqara and Giza indicates that down to the Fourth Dynasty his immediate executives were mainly his close male relatives—sons, uncles, cousins, nephews. In the Fifth Dynasty this ceased to be the case, and high officials, including viziers, were no longer necessarily princes by birth. But even when no longer royal by birth, the men appointed as viziers, and sometimes other officials, were given the rank of prince by the honorific title King's Son. . . .

The King Not a Mere Figurehead

The administrators had the efficient running of Egypt in their hands, and good government was threatened if those administrators sank to the level of bureaucrats. It could happen. Instead of concentrating upon getting necessary work done, officials might act as though what mattered was to adhere at all costs to established procedures, whether or not it was the most efficient way of performing the task in hand. A letter found at Saqqara shows a case of bureaucratic palsy as early as 2200 B.C. The writer was an officer in charge of quarry workers, and obviously a man who took a pride in doing his job well. He expostulated at having been ordered to take his men across the river to government headquarters to receive their clothing, an unwarranted interruption in his duties. In the past, he pointed out, this procedure had wasted up to six days, as a result of delays at the issuing office. Why, he asked, should not the clothes be sent to him by barge, when the whole business could be settled within a single day?

The king himself was not a mere figurehead. Since the earliest viziers were royal princes, there is the possibility that some of those who succeeded as kings may earlier have served in that role. Certainly kings undertook specific functions in the administration of the kingdom. From very early in the Dynastic Period, the king made periodic tours by river to inspect the whole land, and from the reign of the Fourth Dynasty ruler Sneferu, this became a census of all the cattle, normally biennially, occasionally in successive years. This was in effect a periodic assessment of wealth, and must imply the beginning of a national system of taxation. It was this that brought the king the economic power which eventually made possible such huge public works as the building of the Giza pyramids.

From prehistoric times the hydrology of the Nile

had sub-divided Egypt into a number of flood basins. These may have been the basis of the territorial divisions called nomes (totalling about forty, with variations from time to time), which formed the later units of provincial administration. They were already assuming that function by the Third Dynasty, and from soon after that time the administrators in charge of the nomes began to acquire a degree of independence of the capital. In addition, local officials received grants of land for their maintenance, which, in consequence of customarily being regranted to heirs, gradually became treated as private property; with their own estates, such officials became less subject to control from the capital. All this contributed to a weakening of centralized control. The culmination of these trends, combined with other factors which may have included a series of famines resulting from exceptionally low Nile floods, brought a gradual disintegration of the central power, and finally the collapse of the Old Kingdom at the end of the Sixth Dynasty (2155 B.C.).

Ahmose and the Rise of the New Kingdom

Charles Freeman

Egypt's relative isolation from foreign lands ended rather suddenly and boldly with the emergence of the New Kingdom (ca. 1550–1070 B.C.), set in motion by the military victories of Ahmose I. This overview of the New Kingdom's rise, by noted scholar Charles Freeman, tells how foreign invaders called the Hyksos occupied Egypt, how Ahmose drove the intruders out, and how he and his immediate successor revitalized Egypt, building new temples and restructuring the government so that it could efficiently administer Egypt's new and growing empire.

᭠ ᭠ ᭠

The decline of the Middle Kingdom, like that of its predecessor [the Old Kingdom], appears to have been gradual. The Twelfth Dynasty came to an end about 1795 B.C., and then there was a succession of kings with short reigns. Slowly they began losing their grip on the

Charles Freeman, *Egypt, Greece, and Rome: Civilizations of the Ancient Mediterranean*. New York: Oxford University Press, 1996. Copyright © 1996 by Charles Freeman. Reproduced by permission of the publisher.

borders of Egypt. In the eastern Delta there was an influx of migrants from Palestine, which was enjoying a period of particular prosperity. Whether they were actual invaders from a more powerful state or refugees from a time of social upheaval is not clear. The Egyptians called them Hyksos, literally 'chiefs of foreign lands'. By the mid–seventeenth century they were well established enough to take over Memphis and then set up at their own capital at Avaris on the eastern Delta (the site of which, long lost, has now finally been identified). There is evidence that the Hyksos allied themselves with the Nubians in the far south and were thus able to reduce the territory of the Egyptian kings to the land around Thebes. The Middle Kingdom capital Itjtawy was overrun in the early seventeenth century, while in the south the forts on the Nubian frontier appear to have been suddenly abandoned, their garrisons firing them as they left.

Later Egyptian kings talked of the Hyksos as barbarians ('invaders of obscure race who burned our cities ruthlessly, razed to the ground the temples of the gods and treated all the natives with a cruel hostility' was the story passed on by [the Egyptian priest and historian] Manetho). There may be some truth in this. Any intrusion of this nature into the closed world of Middle Kingdom Egypt must have been profoundly disturbing. However, the Hyksos were certainly not uncivilized barbarians determined to destroy the culture of Egypt. With them they brought the harnessed horse, new forms of armour, and weaving on upright looms. Musically they are credited with the introduction of lyres and lutes. Moreover, they were receptive to Egyptian culture, incorporated the name of Ra in their royal titles, and wrote their names in hieroglyphs. They seem to have used Egyptian administrators. They adopted the god Seth [the ambitious and violent usurper of his

brother Osiris's throne], perhaps feeling he best represented their position as outsiders, and worshipped him
alongside their own eastern gods. If anything, the Hyksos period was a time of cultural enrichment for Egypt.

The Victories of Ahmose

In Thebes, meanwhile, a new dynasty emerged—the
Seventeenth. At first its kings seem to have coexisted
with the Hyksos rulers. There is some evidence of trading contacts, and the Hyksos king Apepi may even have
married into the Theban royal family. However, at
some point about 1550 B.C., the Theban kings marched
north. They first broke the links between the Hyksos
and Nubia, then Ahmose I entered the Delta itself, capturing first Memphis, then Avaris, and finally striking
into Palestine itself. The Hyksos were routed. With the
borders secure, Ahmose returned south to restore
Egyptian control over Nubia. The scene was now set
for the New Kingdom, a period of stability which lasted
for 500 years and involved a massive expansion of
Egyptian power into Asia.

With the triumph of Ahmose I of the Eighteenth
Dynasty over the Hyksos, unity and stability returned
to Egypt. There was a very different atmosphere to the
New Kingdom (c. 1550–1070 B.C.). The shock of the
Hyksos incursions had been a profound one for a society as isolated and ordered as Egypt and, in retaliation,
the rulers of the New Kingdom became warrior kings,
building an empire in Asia which at its height reached
as far as the Euphrates. The forces of Seth, normally
seen as undermining the power of the kings, were now
considered to have been subdued by them and redi-
rected at Egypt's enemies. It was Thutmose I (1504–
1492 B.C.) who reached the Euphrates and defeated the
state of Mitanni in Syria. With control established over
the cities of Palestine, local princes, with Egyptian

troops to oversee them, were used to maintain the new empire intact.

Expansion into Other Areas

As in previous dynasties, the kings of the New Kingdom also established firm control over Nubia. Egyptian rule was imposed further south than ever before, down to the Fourth Cataract and probably beyond. A frontier post was established at Napata, under the shadow of a table mountain, Gebel Barkal, which acted as a landmark for traders coming across the desert. For the first time the Egyptians could now directly control the trade routes with their rich harvest of exotic goods coming from central Africa. The Nubian gold mines were also worked so intensively that by the end of the New Kingdom they had become exhausted.

Recently it has been suggested by Martin Bernal in his *Black Athena* that the Egyptian empire also extended into the Mediterranean, with Egypt exercising what he called 'suzerainty' [control] over the Aegean between 1475 and 1375 B.C. (with contact also at earlier periods). So far little evidence has been found to support the argument. Some Egyptian artefacts have been found in the Mediterranean, but hardly enough to support the claim of 'suzerainty'. A survey made in 1987 found a total of only twenty-one artefacts carrying Egyptian royal cartouches, most of these discovered in Crete, the nearest part of the Aegean to Egypt. It seems that many of these may have been traded through the Levantine ports. Egypt had no city on the Mediterranean coast until Alexandria was founded by Alexander the Great in 332 B.C., and no seagoing navy is recorded before the seventh century. It is hard, therefore, to see how Egypt could have maintained any form of control over the Aegean, and Bernal's thesis has received little scholarly support.

It took some time for the New Kingdom to build up

its strength. Despite his military successes, Ahmose of the Eighteenth Dynasty did not reopen the limestone quarries at Tura until late in his reign. His own buildings were all in mudbrick. His successor, Amenhotep I (1525–1504 B.C.), portrayed himself as an aggressive warrior king (one of his names was 'Bull who conquers the lands'), but the evidence is of twenty years of peace and stability. All the usual signs of Egyptian prosperity now returned. New temples were built in Thebes and Nubia, and raw materials started to flow in to support a resurgence of artistic activity. . . .

The Administration of the New Kingdom

[A new system of administering the government also emerged.] The king presided over three departments of government. The first was his own family. This could be large: Ramses II (1279–1213 B.C.), for instance, was said to have fathered 160 children. While the royal family had immense status, not many of its members seem to have been given political power. The king was presumably careful not to encourage those with royal blood to build up positions of influence. There were exceptions, however. The heir might be given command of the army, and there was a traditional role for the queen, or eldest daughter of the king, as Chief Priestess of Amun. (As it was believed that the eldest son of the queen had been conceived in her by Amun, who, by this time, had replaced Ra in this role, this was no more than her due and made her position unassailable.) Through her the king had access to much of the wealth of the temples.

The second department of government oversaw the empire in Nubia and Asia. Apart from Nubia, where the ecology was very similar to what they were used to, the Egyptians were not successful colonizers. Their world was so dependent on the ordered environment of the Nile valley that they found it very difficult to adapt to life outside. When Egyptian armies reached the Euphrates they were completely bewildered by it, never having encountered water flowing southwards. In words reminiscent of the political newspeak of communist China, they described the river as 'water that goes downstream in going upstream'.

Ultimately the Egyptians depended on military force to sustain their rule, and for the first time in Egyptian

---

Ahmose Attacks a Hyksos Stronghold

Egypt's new spirit and policy of military aggression began with Ahmose, who liberated the country. After driving north from Thebes, the pharaoh besieged the main Hyksos stronghold of Avaris, in the eastern section of the Nile Delta. A brief record of this campaign has survived in the tomb biography of the captain of a Nile vessel. His name, like that of his king, was Ahmose.

I showed valor on foot before his majesty; then I was appointed [to be captain of the ship] "Shining-in-Memphis.". . . [I] fought on the water in the canal: Pezedku of Avaris. Then I fought hand to hand, [and] I brought away a hand. [Egyptian soldiers often cut off the hands of slain enemies as battle trophies.] It was reported to the royal herald. [The commander] gave to me the Gold of Valor [a medal for bravery]. . . . Then there was again fighting in this place; I again fought hand to hand there; I brought away [another] hand. [And I received] the Gold of Valor in the second place. . . . [We] captured Avaris; I took captive there one man and three women, a total of four heads [persons]; his majesty gave them to me for slaves.

Quoted in J.H. Breasted, ed., *Ancient Records of Egypt*. 5 vols. New York: Russell and Russell, 1962, vol. 2, pp. 6–7.

history the kings raised a large army, of perhaps between 15,000 and 20,000 men. It was divided into battalions of infantry and charioteers, each battalion fighting under the name of a god. A large proportion of the troops consisted of levies raised within the empire itself. However, the army was expensive and difficult to maintain and soldiering was never popular. In practice most kings contented themselves with punitive raids into Asia or Nubia early in their reigns and then returned to a more settled life in their courts. The normal pattern of administration was indirect, with Egyptian governors, supported by envoys and garrisons, ruling through vassal princes. The governors were responsible for maintaining order and collecting taxes, tribute, and raw materials. Thutmose III, the most successful conqueror of Asia, initiated a policy of bringing back Palestinian princes to Egypt as hostages for the good behaviour of their home cities.

The empire was an important source of raw materials. This had always been the case with Nubia, but Asia also provided booty from the wars and openings for trade. The grain harvests of the plain of Megiddo were appropriated by Thutmose III, tin came from Syria, copper from Cyprus, and silver, valued in Egypt more highly than gold, from Cilicia in southern Anatolia. If the temple inscriptions are to be believed, prisoners were brought back to Egypt in their thousands, and foreigners are to be found as artisans, winemakers, servants, and mercenaries. With them came Asiatic gods and goddesses, among them Astarte, the goddess of horse-riders, who were adopted within the Egyptian pantheon.

The third department of government was concerned with internal administration. This was subdivided into four offices, one each for the administration of the royal estates, the army, the overseeing of religious affairs, and internal civil administration. Each was headed by a small group of advisers, perhaps twenty to thirty at any one time, who were often intimates of the king. The country was divided into two administrative areas, one, Upper Egypt, based on Thebes and the other on Memphis. The success of civil administration was dependent on the personality of the ruler. It was he and only he who could infuse the necessary energy into maintaining the links with the provincial governments stretched out along hundreds of kilometres of valley. Smaller centres had mayors, who were responsible for collecting taxes, probably a tenth of total produce, and carrying out orders from above, although it is not clear how far mayors exercised power over the countryside outside their towns. Criminal cases and the countless property disputes which arose over land which disappeared under water for four months of the year were dealt with by councils of soldiers, priests, and bureaucrats.

Hatshepsut: A Strong Female Monarch

Nicolas Grimal

In this essay, Nicolas Grimal, an Egyptologist at the Sorbonne University in Paris, begins with a brief explanation of the various members of the royal line of Ahmose I, the first pharaoh of the New Kingdom, including Ahmose's son, Amenhotep I. (Note that Grimal uses Amenophis, the accepted alternate version of the name Amenhotep, which means "Amun is content.") From the subsequent marriage of Amenhotep's sister came a daughter—Hatshepsut—who grew to become royal regent and then queen of Egypt. Grimal tells how she managed to gain the throne, no small feat for a woman in ancient times, and how she came to rely on the services of a very talented adviser named Senenmut. He also devotes considerable space to describing the huge and impressive mortuary temple she built at Deir el-Bahri, on the Nile's west bank, opposite Luxor. This structure, her greatest achievement, remains one of the finest examples of ancient Egyptian architecture.

❧ ❧ ❧

Nicolas Grimal, *A History of Ancient Egypt*, translated by Ian Shaw. Oxford, UK: Blackwell, 1992. Copyright © 1992 by Basil Blackwell, Ltd. Reproduced by permission.

As a result of the premature death of Amenophis I's son Amenemhat, it was the descendant of a collateral branch of the family who succeeded him. This man, Tuthmosis I, bolstered his claim to the throne by marrying Ahmes, the sister of Amenophis I. From this union came a daughter, Hatshepsut, and a son, Amenemes. The latter did not reach the throne, but Hatshepsut married her half-brother, the son of Tuthmosis I by a concubine called Mutnofret. Hatshepsut's half-brother and husband eventually became king under the name of Tuthmosis II. The marriage of Tuthmosis II and Hatshepsut failed to produce a male heir; instead they produced another daughter, Neferure. Hatshepsut probably married Neferure to her stepson, Tuthmosis III, who was the son of Tuthmosis II and a royal concubine called Isis.

How Hatshepsut Became Queen

These, broadly speaking, were the successional problems of the descendants of Ahmose. The principle of marriage to a half-sister took place twice to general satisfaction. But in 1479 B.C. Tuthmosis II died—probably through some illness—after only fourteen years on the throne. His son, the future Tuthmosis III, was too young to rule in his own right, therefore Hatshepsut, stepmother of the young Tuthmosis, became regent. The evidence for this regency takes the form of an inscription on a stele in the rock tomb of Inene (Steward of the Granaries of Amun from the reign of Amenophis I to Tuthmosis III) at Sheikh Abd el-Qurna, on the west bank at Thebes:

> [The king] went up to heaven and was united with the gods. His son took his place as King of the Two Lands and he was the sovereign on the throne of his father. His sister, the God's Wife Hatshepsut, dealt

with the affairs of the state: the Two Lands were under her government and taxes were paid to her.

In the second or third year of her regency Hatshepsut abandoned the pretext and had herself crowned as king, with complete titulature [official titles]: Maatkare ('Maat is the *ka* of Ra'), Khnemet-Amun-Hatshepsut ('She who embraces Amun, the foremost of women'). Officially Tuthmosis III was no longer her co-regent. In order to justify this usurpation she effectively ignored Tuthmosis II by inventing a co-regency with her father, Tuthmosis I. She incorporated this fabrication into a group of texts and representations with which she decorated her mortuary temple in the bay of the cliffs at Deir el-Bahri, close to the mortuary temple of the Eleventh Dynasty king Nebhepetre Mentuhotpe II. This 'Text of the youth of Hatshepsut'. . . is both a mythological and a political narrative [described here by scholar Kurt Sethe]:

> In the first scene Amun announces to the Ennead [a group of nine sacred gods] his intention to present Egypt with a new king. Thoth recommends to him Ahmose, the wife of Tuthmosis I. Amun visits her and announces to her that she will give birth to a daughter by him whom she will call 'She who embraces Amun, the foremost of women'. Then, at Ahmose's request, Khnum the potter-god fashions on his wheel the child and her double. Ahmose gives birth to her daughter and presents her to Amun. Amun arranges the education of the child with the help of Thoth and the divine nurse Hathor.
>
> This is followed by scenes of Hatshepsut's coronation. After she has been purified, Amun presents her to the gods of the Ennead. In their company she travels to the north. She is then enthroned by Atum and receives the crowns and royal titles. After being proclaimed king by the gods, she must still be crowned by mankind. Her human father, Tuthmosis

I, introduces her to the royal court, nominates her and has her acclaimed as heir. As soon as her titulature has been announced she undergoes a further rite of purification. . . .

The Queen's Chief Adviser

Hatshepsut reigned until 1458 B.C., the twenty-second year of the reign of Tuthmosis III, who then regained the throne. It seems that during her lifetime she faced less opposition than might have been expected, considering the fury with which her stepson later set out to erase her memory after her death. During her reign she relied on a certain number of prominent figures of whom the foremost was a man called Senenmut. Born of a humble family at Armant, he pursued during Hatshepsut's reign one of the most amazing careers in ancient Egypt. He was 'spokesman' for the queen as well as steward of the royal family and superintendent of the buildings of the god Amun. It was in the latter role that he supervised the transport and erection of the obelisks that the queen installed in the Temple of Amon-Re at Karnak, as well as the construction of her mortuary temple at Deir el-Bahri; in front of this he had a second tomb dug for himself in addition to the one that he already owned at Sheikh Abd el-Qurna.

Even in Senenmut's time there was spiteful gossip suggesting that he owed his good fortune to intimate relations with the queen. In fact it appears that his close connections arose from the role he played in the education of her only daughter Neferure, for whom one of his brothers, Senimen, acted as nurse and steward. Many statues associate the princess with Senenmut, who was a cultured man. His constructions show that he was an architect, but other dimensions of his career are suggested by the presence of an astronomical ceiling in his tomb at Deir el-Bahri and about 150 ostraca in his tomb at Qurna, including several drawings (notably two plans of the tomb itself), as well as lists, calculations, various reports and some copies of religious, funerary and literary texts including *The Satire of the Trades*, *The Tale of Sinuhe* and *The Instruction of Ammenemes I*. Senenmut was a ubiquitous [ever-present] figure throughout the first three-quarters of Hatshepsut's reign, but he subsequently seems to have fallen into disgrace for reasons which are not precisely known. It is thought that after the death of Neferure, which perhaps occurred in the eleventh year of Hatshepsut's reign, he may have embarked upon an alliance with Tuthmosis III which led Hatshepsut to discard him in the nineteenth year of her reign, three years before the disappearance of the queen herself.

Her Greatest Achievement

[Hatshepsut's reign was not marked by great military victories like those of her predecessor Ahmose. Her greatest and most lasting achievement was a magnificent temple.] At Deir el-Bahri Senenmut re-created the basic plan of the temple of Mentuhotpe II and positioned it in relation to the northern enclosure wall of Mentuhotpe's temple. The great originality of Hatshepsut's complex lay in its organization into a succession of terraces in which the changes in plan enabled the monument to harmonize with the natural amphitheatre of the cliffs. The lower (first) terrace was entered through a pylon [large gateway] probably flanked by trees; an axial ramp with colonnades [rows of columns] on either side led up to the middle (second) terrace, raised above the lower one by the height of the colonnades. These colonnades themselves were flanked at their northern and southern ends by colossal Osirid statues. The decoration in the south colonnade showed the erection of the Karnak obelisks, while that in the

The rock-cut tomb and mortuary temple of Hatshepsut, built at Deir el-Bahri, consists of three colonnaded terraces connected by ramps.

north showed scenes of hunting and fishing.

The middle terrace had the same plan as the lower: the south colonnade contained the account of the expedition to the land of Punt [south of Egypt, on the coast of the Red Sea], while the northern colonnade bore scenes of the divine birth and acted as a type of *mammisi* (or divine birth-house). The northern part of the middle terrace provided access to a sanctuary of Anubis [canine god of the dead] with a chapel cut into the cliff. The southern end was bordered by a stepped retaining wall. Between the retaining wall and the enclosure wall a passage, accessible from the lower terrace, led up to a chapel dedicated to Hathor. The second hypostyle hall of this Hathor chapel could be reached directly by way of the colonnade on the uppermost (third) terrace, which was fronted by a peristyle hall. To the north of the peristyle hall was a solar temple consisting of an altar in an open court and a rock-cut chapel in which Tuthmosis I was shown worshipping Anubis. The main sanctuary of the whole temple—cut into the cliff face and flanked by niches containing statues of the queen— consisted of three chapels, the most important of which was the resting place of the sacred bark.

The Queen's Mysterious End

[Though Senenmut no longer advised the queen] the royal entourage still included a High Priest of Amun, a man called Hapuseneb who was related to the royal family through his mother Ahhotep. He was descended from an important family: although his father, Hapu, was only a lector-priest of Amun, his grandfather, Imhotep, had been Tuthmosis I's vizier. Hapuseneb carried out the construction of the temple at Deir el-Bahri and was then awarded the office of High Priest of Amun. He later installed his son as Scribe of the Treasury of Amun.

Another important member of Hatshepsut's court was the Chancellor Nehsy who, in the ninth year of her reign, led an expedition to Punt in a revival of a Middle Kingdom tradition. This expedition, recounted in great detail on the walls of Hatshepsut's mortuary temple, represented the high point of a foreign policy that was limited to the exploitation of the Wadi Maghara mines in Sinai. . . .

[Soon after the expedition to Punt, Hatshepsut disappeared from Egyptian records. It is unknown whether she died of natural causes or was perhaps killed or exiled by her stepson, Tuthmosis III, who became pharaoh. What is certain is that a few years later he ordered her name chiseled off her monuments. However, he could not erase the memory of one of history's first strong female monarchs.]

Thutmose III: The Napoléon of Egypt

Leonard Cottrell

The colorful title conferred on Thutmose III by modern scholars—the Napoléon of Egypt—derives from the fact that he was seen by later generations of Egyptians as the greatest of the warrior pharaohs, those rulers who fought great battles and conquered new territories. He came to power at a time when the New Kingdom was expanding rapidly and creating an empire, mainly in the region of Syria-Palestine; and his victory over the king of Kadesh at Megiddo ensured his country's control of that region. In this summary of Thutmose's reign and achievements, Leonard Cottrell, author of many books about the ancient Near East, begins with the pharaoh's youth, which was spent under the shadow of his stepmother, Queen Hatshepsut. Then Cottrell describes the army Thutmose commanded, which was considerably larger and more lethal than those fielded by the pharaohs in prior ages. This is followed by a general account of the Megiddo campaign and Thutmose's overall legacy.

🐝 🐝 🐝

Astrange and intriguing situation arose at the Theban Court on the death of Tuthmosis II. It can best be illustrated by the fact that in the lists of kings and their reign dates kept by the Egyptians of later times the name Tuthmosis II is followed immediately by that of Tuthmosis III. Yet we know for a certain fact, from other sources, that Tuthmosis III, greatest of all the Warrior Pharaohs, did not rule Egypt as sole monarch until sixteen years later. In the meantime Egypt was governed by Queen Hatshepsut . . . widow of Tuthmosis II and daughter of Tuthmosis I. She was a woman of strong, dominant character. Her nephew (who was also her stepson), Tuthmosis III, was a mere child when Tuthmosis II died, so that according to Ancient Egyptian custom she had the right to reign as regent until the boy came of age. But she so loved authority that she kept Tuthmosis from any active exercise of power until he was at least in his early twenties, long after he should by right have reigned as sole and undisputed king.

As a result of this he hated her and her advisers, especially a certain Sen-en-mut who was her closest friend. Also she must have been very unpopular with the friends of the young king, and most likely the ordinary Egyptian also suspected and distrusted her. For the Egyptians, while they respected and admired their queens, did not want a woman ruling over them in her own right. If she was a queen by virtue of being married to the reigning Pharaoh, that was all right. But Hatshepsut's husband was dead, and though she had royal blood in her veins this did not give her the right to rule if there was a rightful male claimant to the throne. The trouble here was that the young man who became the third Tuthmosis (and the greatest) was not the son of Hatshepsut. His mother was a minor wife of her husband, Tuthmosis II, named Ese (Isis)—the Pharaohs had several wives beside the Queen, who was known as 'Chief Wife'. Because her husband Tuthmosis II was also her half-brother, Hatshepsut was also the third Tuthmosis's aunt, and she became his stepmother after the death of Ese. . . .

Defending the Empire

It is unlikely that the man whom Tuthmosis proved himself to be would have loafed at the Court of Hatshepsut, with Sen-en-mut and her other advisers; he would be more at home with the soldiers with whom he was to campaign for the better part of his reign; and there is a strong suggestion that when he at last came to power he did so with their aid. But equally it would be wrong to think of him necessarily as a young firebrand, itching to unseat his stepmother from the throne in order to fling Egypt into war again. Hatshepsut enjoyed sixteen years of peace, but they had been won for her by her fighting ancestors.

When she disappeared from the scene, in the sixteenth year of the joint reign, Egypt's ancient enemies were again threatening, but this time the danger did not come only from the 'vile Asiatics' [i.e., the Hyksos] whom the Pharaohs had driven from the Nile Valley, but from other, stronger powers which were arising in what are today northern Iraq and Turkey. These were the Mitanni, whose kingdom had been established along the 'Great Bend' of the Euphrates and the much more powerful Hittites of Asia Minor, whom the Egyptians called 'the abominable Kheta'. Neither of these powers threatened Egypt directly, as yet, but they were menacing the Egyptian possessions and subject states in Syria-Palestine. Having won an empire for themselves, the Pharaohs now had to defend it. They were no longer isolated in their valley, content unto themselves. They had become what we call a 'world power', although the civilized 'world' of 1500 B.C. was confined mainly to the east

Mediterranean and the lands to the east of it comprising what geographers used to call the 'Fertile Crescent'. . . .

Not that the Hittites presented an immediate threat to the Egyptians when the young Tuthmosis III, free at last of his stepmother's control, led his armies in the Lebanon and Syria in his first Asiatic campaign. The Hittites were still far off to the north. The immediate enemy were the 'vile Asiatics' led by the King of Kadesh, a powerful, strategically placed city at the northern end of the B'ka Valley in the Lebanon, between twin ranges of mountains. The site is worth memorizing because on more than one occasion it saw much bloodshed. Any army approaching Syria from the south had to pass Kadesh to reach the plains of Syria unless it took the longer coastal route.

Tuthmosis's Army

The army which Tuthmosis III commanded was very different from those of such Middle Kingdom Pharaohs as Senusret and Amenemhat. There were still considerable bodies of infantrymen (foot-sloggers) carrying spears, swords and shields. There were axemen, spearmen and archers, all on foot. But since the rise of the New Kingdom under Ahmose and the first two Tuthmosids there had been what amounted to a revolution in military methods. First, there was now a large regular army organized on a national basis and owing direct allegiance to the king. This army was officered by professional soldiers, not local lords who gave their services and recruited men for the duration of one war.

Secondly, the most important and effective arm was now the chariot force. The chariots were very light, very fast two-wheeled vehicles drawn by swift horses trained for battle. Each chariot carried two warriors, one to drive and the other to hurl spears or shoot from the bow. Approaching out of the sun in a cloud of desert sand, with the combined roar of their massed wheels and galloping hoofs shaking the earth, the Egyptian chariotry were terrifying to the enemy, if well led. They might be approximately compared with the armoured divisions of a modern army with their tanks, half-tracks, armoured cars and so on. . . .

How was this new army organized and officered? At the very top stood the Pharaoh, who usually took the field himself as Commander-in-Chief except in minor campaigns. Next to him in rank was the Vizier, who in civil life might be compared with a Prime Minister, but who was also Minister for War. He was assisted by an Army Council to whom he gave orders. But when campaigning in the field the Pharaoh relied on a council of senior officers whose advice he sought, but did not always follow, as we shall see. The army was organized in divisions consisting of about 5,000 men, each with its divisional commander. These divisions usually had names, so that we read of 'the divisions of Amun, of Re, and Sutekh'—all names of gods. There were also 'second' divisions, probably reserve troops.

Each division, like that of a modern army, was a self-contained unit including both chariotry and infantry, and the divisional commanders were royal princes, except for one division which was usually led by the Pharaoh himself in his war-chariot. Such an army, of upwards of 20,000 men, must have been a splendid sight, whether on the march or deployed in battle array. Under the cloudless sky of Syria, against a background of purple mountains, the mighty host would be seen far off, the sun glinting on the massed spear-heads, on the waving banners of the regiments, and on the gold mountings of the royal and princely chariots. And a great sound would come from it, a mingling of marching feet, rumbling of chariot wheels, clatter of horses' hoofs, and the murmur of many men. . . .

Outfoxing the Enemy

The account of Tuthmosis's victory over the King of Kadesh is recorded in the temple which the Pharaoh erected at Karnak near Luxor. Unlike most such accounts this one appears to be based on first-hand information from an eyewitness; it is less fulsome and vague than other accounts and, in the inscription, the King states that he employed what we would call a 'war correspondent', a scribe whose task was to describe these dramatic events as they happened, on a leather scroll which was deposited in the temple archives. Indeed, we know the actual name of this correspondent, Thaneni, whose tomb on the west shore of Thebes contains the following inscription;

> I followed the Good God, Sovereign of Truth, King of Upper and Lower Egypt, Menkheperre (Tuthmosis III); I beheld the victories of the king which he won in every country. He brought the chiefs of Zahi (in Syria) as living prisoners to Egypt; he captured all their cities. . . . I recorded the victories which he won in every land, putting (them) in writing according to the facts.

The great Annals of Tuthmosis, inscribed on the temple walls, are the world's first full account of a military campaign in which the strategy and tactics of the general in command (Tuthmosis himself) are clearly described. So clearly, in fact, that modern scholars have been able to draw up a plan of battle after carefully examining the ground on which the battle was fought. . . .

Towards the end of the eighth month in his twenty-second year Tuthmosis advanced from his frontier fortress at Tjel (near modern Kantara on the Suez Canal) and crossed the 'Gaza strip' of more recent memory, seizing Gaza, a city of the Philistines, on the anniversary of his accession to the throne of Egypt. Staying only one night in Gaza, which he had reached after a march of ten days, he began another ten-day march to a place called Yehem. . . .

There were three possible approaches through the mountains, two easy but long, one shorter but dangerously narrow, and if the enemy were to come on the Egyptian forces strung out in column-of-route they could be cut to pieces. . . .

[Tuthmosis's officers urged him to take one of the easier roads.] But the young Pharaoh, probably because he had more up-to-date intelligence reports of the enemy's movements, decided to do the one thing which the King of Kadesh would *not* expect him to do, that was to take the narrow, shorter and dangerous road. But first he has to shame his officers into following them. . . . He tells them that he intends to take the Aruna road, the narrow and more difficult (though shorter) one. As for his followers, they may do as they please. . . .

Humbly the officers reply: 'Thy father Amun prosper and thy counsel. Behold we are in the train of Thy Majesty wherever Thy Majesty will go. The servant will follow the master.' Although the Egyptians came under attack as the rearguard had almost reached the end of the defile, the enemy were obviously not expecting Tuthmosis to choose this route. They had expected him to take one of the easier roads, so that when he reached the mouth of the wadi he saw that their south wing was massed at Ta'anach on the edge of the plain, while the north wing was near Megiddo. As so often in warfare, audacity had paid off.

With the Pharaoh's vanguard now beginning to spread out across the plain the officers again address him;

> Behold, His Majesty has come forth together with his victorious army and they have filled the valley; let our victorious lord hearken to us this once, and let our lord await for us the rear of his army and his people. When the rear of the army has come right out to us,

then we will fight against these Asiatics and we shall not have to trouble about the rear of our army.

Tuthmosis Is Victorious

Taking their advice this time, Tuthmosis waits until noon for the rest of the army to come through. Then he advances to the brook Kina, south of Megiddo, by which time it was seven in the evening. . . .

Then comes the account of the battle itself and the famous, oft-quoted description of the king in his armour, mounted on his war-chariot, leading his army into action.

> His Majesty went forth in a chariot of electrum' (alloy of gold and silver) arrayed in his weapons of war, like Horus, the Smiter, lord of power; like Montu of Thebes, while his father, Amun, strengthened his arms. . . .

The description then goes on to explain how the royal army was ordered for battle, with the southern wing on a hill south of the brook Kina, the northern wing at the northwest of Megiddo, while the forces of the centre were led personally by the Pharaoh in his war-chariot. Unfortunately the ancient scribe does not tell us the course of the battle, but only that the Pharaoh won, that he 'prevailed against them'. . . .

Then follows a rebuke to the Egyptian Army for stopping to collect the spoils of battle instead of pursuing the foe in retreat and taking Megiddo.

> Now if only the army of His Majesty had not given their hearts to plundering the things of the enemy, they would have captured Megiddo at this moment, when the wretched foe of Kadesh and the wretched foe of this city were hauled up in haste to bring them into this city. . . .

Tuthmosis, one imagines, was furious;

Then spake His Majesty on hearing the words of his army, saying 'Had you captured this city afterward, behold I would have given (rich treasure) to Re this day; because every chief of every country that has revolted is within it; and because it is the capture of a thousand cities, this capture of Megiddo. Capture ye mightily, mightily. . . .

So Tuthmosis orders a huge wooden wall to be built around Megiddo to prevent anyone escaping. Cedars from the surrounding country must have been felled to build this wall, a big task for the army and one which must have made them regret bitterly not having taken the city at the first onrush when the foe was in retreat. A long siege followed—the wooden wall preventing any possibility of relief from outside, or escape from inside Megiddo, which was eventually starved into surrender. The plunder of the city was considerable, and was carefully itemized in the temple inscription at Karnak, because much of it went as tribute to Amun-Re.

An Inspiration to Later Pharaohs

With Megiddo taken and the enemy defeated or dispersed, Tuthmosis was able to take and plunder other cities in the Lebanon including Yenoam, Nuges, Herenkeru . . . and again follows a careful list of plunder; 1,796 male and female slaves with their children, flat dishes of costly stone and gold, various drinking vessels, gold in rings 'found in the hands of the artificers', a silver statue in beaten work, the head being of gold, chairs, footstools, tables of ivory and carob wood, and so on. The captured land was divided into fields 'which the inspectors of the royal house calculated, in order to reap their harvest'. Then follows a statement of the yield of this harvest, 208,200 fourfold *heket* of grain.

Two facts strike one in reading this and other campaigns recorded in the Annals of Tuthmosis III—seventeen campaigns in all, and all apparently successful. One is that the young Pharaoh showed generalship of a high order, making an unpopular decision and being proved right, and planning his attack in such a way that he chose his own ground and left the enemy at a disadvantage. In all probability the battle was won before a single arrow was fired and Tuthmosis knew this when he arrived on the plain after his hazardous march through the narrow pass, and saw that the enemy, who had expected him by a different route, were disadvantageously placed for a pitched battle; but by then it was too late. . . .

Tuthmosis III has been called 'the Napoleon of Ancient Egypt' with some justice. He was without doubt the most brilliant fighting general she ever produced, and his example inspired some of his great successors such as Sethi I, and Ramesses II and III. Although we have to rely for most of our information on the stilted priestly chronicles, concerned more with recording the loot for the temple of Amun-Re than describing the Pharaoh's personality and achievements, a hint here and there suggests a generous, warm-hearted as well as a brave and skilful man. His record is not stained with massacres and other atrocities; he frequently shows mercy to the inhabitants of captured towns, and his troops evidently adored him, to judge by the way they followed him loyally almost to the ends of what to them was the world. It took a great deal of courage for the Ancient Egyptian, accustomed for some 1,500 years to the closed society of the Nile Valley, to venture out into the high mountains of Syria, and even to cross the mysterious Euphrates, which, contrary to the Nile, flowed southwards instead of northward. So they had to give it the quaint title of 'the river which in flowing southward flows northward'.

Tuthmosis acquired a number of foreign wives from Asia, including three princesses bearing the charming names of Menhet, Menwi and Merti. Some years ago 'illicit diggers' operating near Luxor found their tomb, and robbed it, feeding the 'grave-goods' on to the market at intervals. Among these objects are three sets of toilet articles of gold, silver and other precious materials now on view at the Metropolitan Museum of Art, New York. . . . As far as we know, the only woman he thoroughly detested was his aunt and stepmother Hatshepsut. After her death he defaced her monuments, cutting out her sculptured reliefs wherever he found them, defacing her royal name and substituting either his own or those of his predecessors Tuthmosis I and II. He even desecrated the tombs of her favourites, especially that of Sen-en-mut. But no doubt he had very good reasons for this hatred.

So it was that in later times even the records of this queen's reign as regent to Tuthmosis were obliterated, and instead the name of Tuthmosis II is followed, on the records, by that of Tuthmosis III, 'Menkheperre, the scourge of the Asiatics'.

Hymn of Victory for Thutmose III

Priests of Amun

Toward the end of the eventful reign of Thutmose III, some priests of the god Amun composed the following hymn, which they claimed was inspired by the god himself. This piece of propaganda celebrates the pharaoh's many military victories, lists the enemies he has overcome or intimidated, and in general validates Thutmose's policy of naked conquest.

Thou comest to me, thou exultest [rejoice], seeing
    my beauty,
O my son, my avenger . . . , living for ever.
I have given to thee might and victory against all
    countries.
I have set thy fame, even the fear of thee, in all lands,
Thy terror as far as the four pillars of heaven.
I have felled thine enemies beneath thy sandals.
My serpent diadem [crown] gives light to thy dominion.
There is no rebel of thine as far as the circuit of heaven;

The Priests of Amun, "Utterance of Amon-Re, Lord of Thebes," *Never to Die: The Egyptians in Their Own Words*, edited by Josephine Mayer and Tom Prideaux. New York: Viking, 1938.

They come, bearing tribute upon their backs,
Bowing down to thy majesty according to my
command.
I have made powerless the invaders who came before
thee;
Their hearts burned, their limbs trembled.

I have come, causing thee to smite the eastern land,
Thou hast trampled those who are in the districts of
God's-Land.
I have caused them to see thy majesty like a circling star,
When it scatters its flame in fire, and gives forth its dew.

I have come, causing thee to smite the western land,
Keftyew [the Greek island of Crete] and Cyprus are in
terror.
I have caused them to see thy majesty as a young bull,
Firm of heart, ready-horned, irresistible.

I have come, causing thee to smite those who are in
their marshes,
The lands of Mitanni [a kingdom lying east of Syria]
tremble under fear of thee.
I have caused them to see thy majesty as a crocodile,
Lord of fear in the water, unapproachable.

I have come, causing thee to smite those who are in the
isles;
Those who are in the midst of the Great Green hear
thy roarings,
I have caused them to see thy majesty as an avenger
Who rises upon the back of his slain victim.

I have come, causing thee to smite the Libyans,
The isles of Utentyew are subject to the might of thy
prowess.

I have caused them to see thy majesty as a fierce-eyed
    lion
That maketh them corpses in their valleys.

I have come, causing thee to smite the uttermost ends of
    the lands,
The circuit of the Great Circle is enclosed in thy grasp.
I have caused them to see thy majesty as a lord of the
    wing,
Who seizeth upon that which he seeth, as much as he
    desires.

I have come, causing thee to smite those who are in
    front of their land,
Thou hast smitten the Sand-dwellers [desert tribesmen]
    as living captives.
I have caused them to see thy majesty as a southern
    jackal,
Lord of running, stealthy-going, who roves the Two
    Lands [i.e., Egypt].

I have come, causing thee to smite the Nubian
    Troglodytes [lowly cave dwellers; a standard insult
    against Nubians],
As far as Shat they are in thy grasp.
I have caused them to see thy majesty as thy two
    brothers.
I have united their two arms for thee in victory.
Thy two sisters, I have set them as protectors behind
    thee,
The arms of my majesty are above, warding off evil.

I have caused thee to reign, my beloved son,
Horus, Mighty Bull, shining in Thebes,
Whom I have begotten, in uprightness of heart.
Thutmose, living for ever.

Amenhotep III: A Colossal Builder

Betsy M. Bryan

This overview of what is known about the prominent New Kingdom pharaoh Amenhotep III, father of the famous heretic pharaoh Akhenaten (Amenhotep IV), is by Johns Hopkins University scholar Betsy M. Bryan. First, Bryan discusses Amenhotep's family and boyhood and suggests that he knew Tiye, who soon became Queen Tiye, his principal wife, at an early age. Next, Bryan explores the theory that Amenhotep's preoccupation with the sun and deities associated with the sun had an important influence on Akhenaten, who later worshipped the sun's disk, which he called the Aten. In particular, Bryan examines Amenhotep's impressive building programs, including temples, forts, and colossal statues, among the largest ever built in Egypt. The essay also makes the point that Amenhotep's reign was largely a time of peace and prosperity in which Egypt's ruler carried on vigorous correspondence and other diplomatic relations with foreign lands.

🐝 🐝 🐝

Betsy M. Bryan, "The 18th Dynasty Before the Amarna Period (c. 1550–1352 B.C.)," *The Oxford History of Ancient Egypt*, edited by Ian Shaw. Oxford, UK: Oxford University Press, 2000. Copyright © 2000 by Oxford University Press. Reproduced by permission.

The thirty-eight-year reign of Amenhotep III was primarily a period of peace and affluence. The construction of royal monuments during the reign was on a scale with few parallels, and the retinue [courtiers] of the king left tombs, statues, and shrines that rivalled those of many former rulers. Sadly, as in most periods, it is impossible to compare the fortunes of the rich with those of the poor. Whether the peasant's life was economically improved due to the overall wealth in Egypt is unknown. The official documentation might suggest that the population as a whole enjoyed prosperity at some point, since Amenhotep III and his granary official Khaemhet boasted of the 'bumper' crop of grain harvested in the king's crucial jubilee year 30. The king was remembered even 1,000 years later as a fertility god, associated with agricultural bounty. Still, this type of evidence is hardly unbiased, so we must admit our ignorance.

It is probable that Amenhotep III was a child at his accession. A statue of the treasurer Sobekhotep holding a prince Amenhotep-mer-khepesh probably shows the king shortly before his father's death, and a wall painting in the tomb of the royal nurse Hekarnehhe describes the tomb-owner as the royal nurse of Prince Amenhotep, portraying the prince as a youth rather than a small naked child. The age of the king at accession could have been anywhere between 2 and 12, with a later age perhaps to be preferred given that Amenhotep's mother, Mutemwiya, was barely more visible than Tiaa and Merytra, the preceding two kings' mothers. A regency by Mutemwiya appears unlikely, and, if the king was indeed a small child at accession, his rule was conducted for him quite unobtrusively. An alternative possibility might be that members of Queen Tiye's family assisted the king in his early rule. A scarab dated in year 2 of Amenhotep's reign established the early date of his marriage to Tiye, and the identification on another scarab of the queen's parents, Yuya and Tuya, underscores their prominence. There is, at present, no documentary evidence that Tiye's family acted as a power behind the throne. . . .

The Divinity of Amenhotep III

Recent discussions of the reign of Amenhotep III have suggested that he was deified during his lifetime, not only in Nubia, where he built a cult temple for himself, but also in Egypt proper. [Scholar] Raymond Johnson has argued that Amenhotep III's insistent identification with the sun-god in his monumental iconography and inscriptions should be understood as his deification, and he further contends that Amenhotep IV/Akhenaten (1352–1336 B.C.) transformed his deified father into the disembodied solar disc Aten, thereby worshipping the living Amenhotep III as the sole god of the world. The view that Amenhotep IV worshipped his father as the Aten (albeit after his death) [is intriguing]. . . .

It is arguable that Amenhotep III intended to be identified with the sun-god from the time of his first jubilee in years 30–31, since scenes representing that festival show him taking the specific role of Ra riding in his solar boat. The degree to which Amenhotep III was associated with the sun-god on monuments might well have encouraged the view that, having merged with the sun, as the king was expected to do after death, he was present in Akhenaten's deity, the solar disc Aten. . . .

It is also noteworthy that Amenhotep III named his own palace complex 'the gleaming Aten' and used stamp seals for commodities that may be read 'Nebmaatra [his prenomen] is the gleaming Aten'. Of course, sealings are economic documents and could as such refer to the palace complex itself; they might, therefore, have been intended to be read as 'the gleaming Aten of Nebmaatra'. What is certain is that the association of the Aten with Amenhotep III was well established in his own documentation prior to the reign of Amenhotep IV/Akhenaten.

It is impossible at this point to prove or disprove Johnson's argument. There are no stelae or statues that were, with certainty, dedicated to Amenhotep III as a major deity within Egypt in his lifetime—much less as the Aten. . . .

After years of debate, we are no closer to a resolution of the debate about . . . the deification of Amenhotep III as the Aten. It might not be unfair to suggest, however, that Amenhotep III would have been pleased that, 3,350 years after his death, it is difficult to ascertain whether he ruled as a living god or merely strived to give that impression. . . .

The Building Programme of Amenhotep III

Amenhotep III's building programme gave him space to design an eternal divinity for himself. . . . He consistently identified himself with the national deities, not his deceased royal predecessors, and he represented himself as the substitute for major gods in a few instances. In addition, his buildings document an unparalleled emphasis on solar theology, such that the cults of Nekhbet, Amun, Thoth, and Horus-khenty-khety, for example, were heavily solarized during Amenhotep III's reign. Trends apparent in 18th Dynasty funerary literature reveal that the sun's cyclicity and its potential for fertility or famine were manifest in the world and in the ruler, but monuments and objects made in Amenhotep III's time may have disseminated these notions more widely. . . .

Amenhotep built temples or shrines in Nubia at Quban, Wadi es-Sebua, Sedeinga, Soleb, and Tabo Island. There are building elements or stelae in his name at Amada, Aniba, Buhen, Mirgissa, and Gebel Barkal (perhaps reused in the latter). There are statues or scarabs in his name at a variety of sites, including Gebel Barkal and Kawa, and most of the statues originated at other sites, particularly at Soleb. In Egypt proper the king built a shrine at Elephantine (now destroyed) and completed a chapel at Elkab, probably partially erected by his father. Some 20 km. south of Thebes Amenhotep III built a temple at Sumenu, site of a cult to the crocodile Sobek. Although the temple itself remains elusive, numerous objects from it and the cemetery associated with its town, have come to light since the 1960s.

It is in Thebes that Amenhotep's penchant for the colossal is most visible today. The Colossi of Memnon were the towering quartzite images of Amenhotep that protected the king's first pylon at his funerary temple (the single largest royal temple known from ancient Egypt). More fragments of colossal sculpture have been found within his mortuary temple than in any other known sacred precinct. Buildings on the east bank of the Nile at Thebes included a series of constructions at Karnak, as well as Luxor temple, which was entirely rebuilt. . . .

On the west bank of Thebes, south of the king's enormous funerary temple, was located his enormous palace of 'the gleaming Aten', now termed Malkata after the Arabic designation for the Queen's Valley nearby. Still further south, at Kom el-Samak, the king built a jubilee pavilion of painted mud brick. A Japanese expedition excavated and carefully recorded this building, which is now destroyed. Next to the Malkata complex is the great harbour that Amenhotep created for use during his constructions and habitation at the palace. . . .

The work of Amenhotep III at Karnak, Luxor, and his funerary temple reveals his interest in stressing the royal identification with the sun-god. After completing the monuments of his father, Thutmose IV, he changed the face of the Karnak temple. At some undetermined point in his reign, Amenhotep III's workers dismantled the peristyle court in front of the Fourth Pylon and the shrines associated with it, using them as fill for a new pylon, the Third, on the east-west axis. This created a new entrance way to the temple, and two rows of columns with open papyrus capitals were erected down the centre of the newly formed forecourt. He also began the construction of the Tenth Pylon at the south end of Karnak, changing its orientation slightly from that of the Seventh and Eighth in order that it led to a new entrance for the precinct of the goddess Mut, for whom he may also have built or begun a temple. Balancing the south-temple complex was a new building to the north of central Karnak, which was a shrine to the goddess Maat, the daughter of the sun-god. Both Mut and Maat could represent the solar eye of Ra, his agent in the world. [Archaeologist] David O'Connor has

The towering sandstone Colossi of Memnon, located at Luxor, were just one of Amenhotep III's many building projects.

noted that the north-south opposition corresponds to heavenly and terrestrial settings, a fact that accords well with the divine roles of Maat and Mut respectively. The rituals and offerings that Amenhotep III provided may have been designed to demonstrate architecturally and inscriptionally his ability, like the sun-god, to create stability in the cosmos. Deeply carved reliefs from a granary within Karnak show the king in elaborate regalia, crowned with multiple solar discs, and bejewelled on his kilt apron and body with solar imagery. In addition, the king's face is childlike, and his body type is thicker and shorter waisted than on most of the temple reliefs. This is a rejuvenated Amenhotep III, who also exhibits the jubilee iconography with elaborated divine, and particularly solar, elements. . . .

The royal penchant for ritual drama was further monumentalized in Amenhotep III's funerary temple. The temple contained large numbers of life-sized and colossal statuary in the form of both well-known and obscure deities, frequently with human bodies topped by animal heads. These statues represented both the gods of the jubilee and a three-dimensional astronomical calendar to guarantee a propitious festival year. . . .

International Relations in the Reign of Amenhotep III

A Nubian campaign took place in year 5 of Amenhotep III's reign. . . . The building of the fortress of Khaemmaat at Soleb, where the king also constructed a temple, may have been intended to prevent further disruptions from Upper Nubia. The earlier Upper Nubian capital at Kerma was almost directly across the river from Soleb, so the site may have been chosen to underscore Kushite subjection to Egypt.

International relations with the rest of the ancient world were conducted through diplomatic missions. The amount of Egyptian material on the Greek mainland increased dramatically in the reign of Amenhotep III, and the names of Aegean cities, including Mycenae, Phaistos, and Knossos, appear for the first time in hieroglyphic writing on statue bases from the king's funerary temple. Letters between Amenhotep III and several of his peers in Babylon, Mitanni, and Arzawa are preserved in cuneiform writing on clay tablets. These letters, many found in the archive of Akhenaten's capital of Amarna, demonstrate the powerful position enjoyed by Amenhotep III as he negotiated to marry the daughters of other rulers. A strong connection between Amenhotep III and the Mitanni king Tushratta is apparent in the letters, while the Babylonian king Burnaburiash, who came to power late in Amenhotep's rule, appears more suspicious of Egyptian strength. The mid–14th century B.C. certainly represents one of the high points of Egypt's influence in the ancient world, and it was the culmination of activities by nearly all the rulers of the 18th Dynasty.

Profiles · in · History

Akhenaten: The Heretic Pharaoh

Akhenaten and His Religious Revolution

Lionel Casson

Scholars and nonscholars alike have long been fascinated by one of the most unusual and compelling figures of the ancient world—the tenth pharaoh of Egypt's New Kingdom, Amenhotep IV, better known as Akhenaten. During his tumultuous reign (lasting from about 1352 to 1336 B.C.), he overthrew existing religious and artistic traditions and devoted himself and his considerable resources as pharaoh to the worship of Aten—the sun's disk. At his death, the priests and most other leading Egyptians reversed his revolution, reasserted the priority of the traditional pantheon of gods, and attempted to erase his name from the annals of history. (Luckily for posterity, they failed.) Modern historians have advanced numerous theories to explain the motivations for Akhenaten's heretical beliefs and actions; and some of the better known of these proposals are summarized in this illuminating essay by Lionel Casson, one of the leading classical historians of the twentieth century.

🐦 🐦 🐦

Lionel Casson, *Daily Life in Egypt*. New York: American Heritage, 1975. Copyright © 1975 by American Heritage Publishing Company, Inc. All rights reserved. Reproduced by permission.

About 1400 B.C. Amenhotep III ascended the throne. He carried on his predecessors' vigorous way of life only to the extent of going after big game (he boasts of bagging a grand total of 102 lions), leaving the leading and exercising of the troops to others. . . . His ancestors had gained and maintained Egypt's empire by the force of her arms; Amenhotep maintained it by her gold and prestige. He made alliances with the neighboring rulers in Syria, the Levant, Mesopotamia, and Asia Minor and cemented them by means of gifts and marriages, adding their sisters and daughters to his harem; he was negotiating for yet another Asiatic bride shortly before he died, an old and ailing man whose reign had lasted thirty-eight years.

The one activity he did indulge in was building. . . . Deep in the Sudan below the Third Cataract he built a temple for himself and Amon and not far away another for Tiy, his queen; despite her nonroyal birth and despite the Asiatic ladies of lofty pedigree in his harem, he was devoted to his Great Wife, associated her with the important affairs of state, and lavished gifts on her, even going as far as to dig her a private lake. During the last years of his life he may have adopted his eldest son, Amenhotep IV, as coregent; perhaps he wanted to shuck off all cares of state and devote himself full time to his building and his harem. As it happened, the son's coronation, whether as coregent or as pharaoh in his own right at the old man's death, opened a unique and most strange period in Egyptian history.

Breaking with Tradition

At the outset all seemed normal enough. He took a wife, Nefertiti, and she promptly bore him the first of six daughters. He had himself portrayed in the time-honored fashion of the pharaohs, with trim athletic figure in a regal pose. Within a short time, however, it became patently clear that the new king had ideas very much his own. He began to evince a marked disinterest in Amon, the dynasty's pampered patron deity, and a marked interest in the Aten, the sun disk. In doing so he was on well-trodden ground, venturing into nothing unorthodox. Re, god of the sun, was . . . one of the oldest and most respected Egyptian deities; the Aten was simply his visible aspect, and three generations of pharaohs had already turned it into an object of worship of high standing. Amenhotep III, for all his manifest predilection for Amon, had named his flagship the *Splendor of Aten.*

But his son's devotion, it quickly transpired, was of a different order. Not very long after gaining the throne, he put up a temple for the Aten just east of Amon's vast complex at Karnak, and in its court he included a series of colossal statues of himself that must have hit contemporaries like a thunderbolt, so violent was their break with the past. Such statues of previous pharaohs had always represented them either in jubilee costume or in mummy wrappings as resurrected immortals, assimilated to Osiris, king of the underworld. Amenhotep IV chose to represent himself as a living king in the costume of the living and to add inscriptions pointing to an assimilation with the Aten and not Osiris.

Even more iconoclastic [nontraditional], instead of representing himself in the traditional heroic fashion, he had his sculptors give him an elongated jaw, scrawny neck, drooping shoulders, potbelly, spindly shanks, and buttocks as thick and rounded as a woman's. As if to underline this feminine aspect, in the statues of him nude, he had them show him without genitalia. . . . The nineteenth-century archaeologists who discovered them were convinced they were dealing with representations of a woman, some queen. When the deciphering of the inscriptions revealed beyond any doubt that the subject was a pharaoh, Auguste Mariette, the great French Egyptologist, suggested that perhaps the poor fellow had been captured while campaigning in the Sudan and castrated, with the effects visible in his statues. . . .

A New Capital City

In the sixth year of his reign, the young pharaoh made another, even more startling break. The Aten was his deity, not Amon; he was no more able to feel at ease in Thebes, under the shadow of Amon's awesome and sumptuous temples at Karnak and Luxor. . . . So he abandoned Thebes and set up a new capital at a place called today Tell el Amarna, some 250 miles downriver. He gave it the name Akhetaten, "the Horizon of the Aten," and at the same time changed his own name from Amenhotep to Akhenaten, "the Effective Spirit of the Aten." The Aten, in other words, was to be the official god of the land.

We know the new city better than any other in Egypt because after Akhenaten died in dishonor it was abandoned, to lie forgotten and undisturbed under a blanket of sand until archaeology began its resurrection at the end of the last century. Though Akhenaten's enemies had sown destruction with religious zeal, enough was left to reveal a well-planned complex. At its heart was a great temple to the Aten, which, in dramatic contrast to Amon's, was open, bathed in the sun's light. Surrounding it were the royal palace, administration buildings, an elegant residential section for members of the court, a humbler area for the rank and file, workshops, and so on. The cliffs roundabout were honeycombed with elaborate tombs. . . .

In his new capital Akhenaten was free to worship as he liked. A hymn, presumably from his own hand, was found inscribed on the wall of a tomb belonging to one of his high officials. In it the king addresses his new god, in lofty and fervent phrases. It reveals a vision of a brave new world in which a single deity would replace the swarm that inhabited Egypt, above all would replace Amon. Beliefs from Amarna show the Aten with rays that end in hands stretching downward toward Akhenaten and his family, while any courtiers who are about bow reverently and humbly. Akhenaten, in other words, prayed to the Aten, and everyone else prayed to Akhenaten; there was no god but the one god, and Akhenaten was the sole entrée to him. At some point Akhenaten translated his egocentric monotheism into effective action: he sent men forth armed with mallets and chisels to strike out the offending name of Amon wherever they found it, whether on vast temples or tiny scarabs, whether in the heart of Thebes or deep in the Sudan. He even had them strike out such terms as "the gods."

Art Reflects the King's Worldview

Since most of what we know about Akhenaten's career comes from the archaeological record and very little from inscriptions or archives—we have a limited amount of such material from Egypt in general, and in the great heretic's case, whatever there was must have been systematically destroyed—the most obvious manifestation of his revolutionary regime is its art, the style that produced with such dramatic suddenness the monumentally ugly and distorted statues in his temple to the Aten. The Amarna style, as it is called, since the new capital was where it reached full bloom, is characterized by a departure from Egypt's rigid artistic ways toward a greater freedom and naturalism: the artists show figures in lifelike movement, in natural groupings, in easy poses. Actually, the beginnings of this art predate Akhenaten, for a certain amount of naturalism had made its appearance during the reigns of his predecessors; now, however, it comes strikingly to the fore. Poses and movements that artists previously had reserved only for minor figures—for dwarfs, dancers, yokels—are now given to the king and his family. Instead of the traditional static and formal court scenes, we get representations of the king munching on a bone or nuzzling his children, the queen dandling them on her lap, a pair of princesses lounging on cushions. Instead of a traditional heroic pharaoh, we get Akhenaten as he presumably looked, eggheaded, potbellied, spindly shanked. But the artists swiftly move from naturalism to mannerism—they give the whole family the very same set of characteristics. And the royal family's portraits in turn set a fashion: members of the court dutifully instruct their painters and sculptors to make them look like the pharaoh. These grotesqueries are the unmistakable mark of the years of the great heresy. As might be expected, Akhenaten's successors ostentatiously returned to Egypt's traditional artistic as well as religious ways.

Besides art, another source of information about the nature of the heresy is the *Hymn of Akhenaten*, a copy of which was found inscribed in the tomb of one of his devoted adherents. In it the king addresses the Aten as the sole god, creator of all life, protector of the whole world:

> Thou appearest beautifully on the horizon of
>   heaven,
> Thou living Aten, the beginning of life! . . .

One god, creator of all living things, of all beasts and all men—such a concept was as much a departure from traditional Egyptian religion as the Amarna style was from traditional art.

Popular Theories About Akhenaten
What manner of man was this so un-Egyptian Egyptian who found a need to launch a new direction in art, who had the vision to conceive of an exalted monotheism, the

zeal to strike down a religion hallowed by time, the megalomania to set himself up as the sole intermediary between god and man? The question has teased Egyptologists ever since the strange interlude that he created in Egyptian history first came to be known. They have picked over all the scraps of information we have about him in an effort to come upon some cogent explanation. Unfortunately there are only a mere handful, of which most are more tantalizing than informative. And so, over the years, a whole series of Akhenatens have emerged, each reflecting the writer's predilections and prejudices.

James Henry Breasted, for decades the leading figure in Chicago's Oriental Institute, was enthralled by the revolutionary pharaoh. He idolized this "lonely idealist of the Fourteenth Century before Christ," endowing him with a sensitive love of light and of nature, . . . with a universal humanitarianism, . . . with a profound and creative religious vision. He was passionately convinced that Akhenaten, a "god-intoxicated" man, was the true father of monotheism. . . . Breasted painted a picture of his hero that is absorbing and exhilarating—but . . . [without] much basis in fact.

Balancing Breasted's religious visionary is the political and social reformer conjured up by a school infected with Marxist ideals. Akhenaten's creation of a new god and his retirement from Thebes, in their view, were moves in a class struggle, with the idealistic pharaoh upholding the cause of those under the heel of the entrenched interests. Heading a group of self-made men, he challenged the traditional ruling families and the traditional ideology, only to fall before an alliance of the army and reactionary clergy, particularly the priesthood of Amon, which was frantically eager to regain its lost power and revenues. It is a script no less imaginative than Breasted's.

One side of Akhenaten that has exercised a particular

fascination has been the grotesque appearance he made his portraitists record so carefully. Was it pure affectation on his part to have himself pictured that way? Or did he actually look like that? And if so, what effect did it have on his ideals, on his chosen activities, since obviously no one of such a physique could possibly cast himself in the role of a conqueror like Thutmose III or a hunter and athlete like Amenhotep II. This is a point on which doctors presumably might have something to say, and several of them did. They pointed out that there is a pituitary disorder called Fröhlich's syndrome that produces symptoms remarkably similar to the features visible in Akhenaten's portraits: distortion of the skull, excessive growth of the jaw, plumping out of the abdomen and buttocks and thighs, overly slender lower limbs, corpulence, and infantile genitalia, at times so embedded in fat as to be invisible. It sounds convincing—until we remember that victims of the ailment are impotent, whereas Akhenaten presumably fathered at least six daughters. A few historians, determined to salvage the enticing medical explanation at any price, convinced themselves that, in the reliefs showing Akhenaten fondling his babes, the pharaoh doth protest too much; they suggest that his father, who was still collecting recruits for his harem when well on in years, may have solved the son's embarrassing position by doing the sexual honors for him. . . .

Akhenaten the Individualist?

In 1951 the late John Wilson, one of Breasted's successors at the Oriental Institute, gave a reconstruction of Akhenaten's reign that emphasized its manifest connections with the mainstream of Egyptian history. As he saw it, Akhenaten was independent-minded and avantgarde, sensitively responsive to the new currents that had been generated by Egypt's transformation to an international power. A freer, more naturalistic movement in art had already begun during his father's reign, and he favored it. A movement had gotten under way to flavor the rigidly stiff and formal traditional language with more up-to-date expressions, foreign borrowings, even colloquialisms, and he favored that. Above all he favored a new way of religion.

This religion was by no means totally novel; indeed, many of its ideas and modes of expression had been current before his time and after his excommunication would live on for centuries and ultimately affect Hebrew literature. However, his particular version definitely put him at odds with the powerful clerical establishment of the prevailing church, Amon's.

When his father died, the young thinker was free to put into effect the ideas that he had been germinating. He now began to order his artists to use the style that we always associate with him, one which, though based on the naturalistic movement already well under way, pushed it to extremes—as we know from his own statements, he treasured truth above all, and it follows that he would seek truth in art, portrayals of himself as he actually looked, pictures of himself in scenes that actually took place. After six years at Thebes, stronghold of the priests of Amon, who must have bitterly opposed him, he gathered together a coterie of devoted adherents front families of no particular standing—they recorded in their tomb inscriptions their heartfelt thanks to the pharaoh for their rise from nothing—and transferred to a new capital where he could implement his revolutionary ideas undisturbed. But the tide began to set against him. Even his idyllic family life was affected: Nefertiti was banned from the main palace—we find her name erased there and replaced by her eldest daughter's—to a residence at the northern end of town. He decided upon his younger brother, Smenkhare, as heir apparent, married him to his eldest daughter, and used him as go-between for a compromise with his enemies—there is evidence that the young man returned to Thebes and resumed relations there with Amon. Nefertiti, however, remained stubbornly devoted to the cause of revolution, and she must have kept the boy Tutankhamen, who was in line to succeed to the throne after Smenkhare, in her clutches, for their names appear together in her new dwelling.

Eventually both Akhenaten and Smenkhare disappear from the scene, probably carried off by death; Tutankhamen ascends the throne, and, bowing to the forces about him, engineers a return to the *status quo ante* [way things were before]. This is a persuasive reconstruction—but still just a reconstruction, based largely on inference from a word here, a picture there, an erasure in another place, and so on.

No Place for Mavericks

Yet another reconstruction has been offered by Cyril Aldred, who argues that there was no opposition between Akhenaten and the priesthood of Amon; in Egypt the pharaoh *was* the church, so Akhenaten very likely transported Amon's priests to serve his new god in the new capital. He argues that Akhenaten was not surrounded by parvenus [social climbers] but by the younger sons of the nobility; their fulsome thanks for being raised from nothing were merely a novel way of flattering a pharaoh. Most important, he argues that for the better part of his reign Akhenaten was content to leave Egypt's other deities alone; it was only in the last five years, when in quick succession he lost the people nearest and dearest to him—two daughters, a beloved son-in-law, his wife (this is why her name was erased), his mother—that something gave way and he unleashed his fury on Amon and the rest of Egypt's pantheon.

Thus Aldred, though working with the same scraps of information as Wilson, makes them yield a considerably different story. [More recently, still another theory about Akhenaten was proposed by scholar C.N. Reeves. He contends that the heretic pharaoh launched his religious revolution as a play to gain more political power for the throne.]

Ancient Egypt, with its age-old dedication to tradition, was no place for mavericks. Akhenaten was the only one in the long list of its royalty, and his successors did their best to rewrite Egypt's records and leave him out. In the official list of pharaohs, Haremhab's first year begins right after Amenhotep III's last, neatly consigning to oblivion all the rulers tainted with heresy— Akhenaten, Smenkhare, Tutankhamen. It has been the Egyptologists who have resurrected Akhenaten, exhuming his capital from the sands, extracting remains of his buildings at Thebes from the walls of later structures for which they had been cannibalized, deciphering the inscriptions left by him and his officials, making what inferences they could from his portraits and court scenes. But, barring a phenomenal piece of luck, except for stray bits of information that archaeology may produce, we very likely will never know much more about him than we do now. And this means that the answer to the seductive question of what made him a maverick will forever remain guesswork. Was he an inspired visionary? convinced but misguided reformer? megalomaniac? madman? Take your pick—or, if you prefer, wait for further choices; that these will be forthcoming is the one thing about Akhenaten we may be sure of.

The Great Hymn to Aten

Akhenaten

One of the most important and revealing of Akhenaten's legacies turned out to be the Great Hymn to Aten (or Aton), a glorification of the god thought to have been composed by the pharaoh himself (although there is no way to be certain he is the sole author). A work of true beauty and serenity, as well as deep religious devotion, it has often been compared to the Hebrew Psalms, which glorify the Judeo-Christian God with similar phrases.

❦ ❦ ❦

You rise in perfection on the horizon of the sky,
living Aten, who started life.
Whenever you are risen upon the eastern horizon
you fill every land with your perfection.
You are appealing, great, sparkling, high over every
    land;
your rays hold together the lands as far as everything
    you have made.
Since you are Re, you reach as far as they do,

Akhenaten, "The Hymn to Aten," *The Literature of Ancient Egypt: An Anthology of Stories, Instructions, and Poetry*, edited by W.K. Sampson. New Haven, CT: Yale University Press, 1973.

and you curb them for your beloved son.
Although you are far away, your rays are upon the
    land;
you are in their faces, yet your departure is not
    observed.
Whenever you set on the western horizon,
the land is in darkness in the manner of death.
They sleep in a bedroom with heads under the covers,
and one eye does not see another.
If all their possessions which are under their heads
    were stolen,
they would not know it.
Every lion who comes out of his cave and all the
    serpents bite,
for darkness is a blanket.
The land is silent now, because he who made them
is at rest on his horizon.

But when day breaks you are risen upon the horizon,
and you shine as the Aten in the daytime.
When you dispel darkness and you give forth your
    rays
the two lands are in festival,
alert and standing on their feet,
now that you have raised them up.
Their bodies are clean,/and their clothes have been
    put on;
their arms are lifted in praise at your rising.

The entire land performs its work:
all the cattle are content with their fodder,
trees and plants grow,
birds fly up to their nests, their wings extended in
    praise for your Ka [personal life force].
All the kine [cattle] prance on their feet;
everything which flies up and alights,

they live when you have risen for them.
The barges sail upstream and downstream too,
for every way is open at your rising.
The fishes in the river leap before your face
when your rays are in the sea.

You who have placed seed in woman
and have made sperm into man,

A Modern Recording of Aten's Hymn

No one knows for sure if the Hymn to Aten was originally chanted or sung; whether it was performed by
solo voice or choir; or whether it was accompanied by
musical instruments. More than three thousand years
later, Akhenaten's beautiful tribute to his god was re-
vived in a splendid manner as part of the musical
score for Twentieth Century Fox's lavish 1954 film,
The Egyptian. The plot revolves around an Egyptian
doctor, Sinuhe, who becomes court physician and
friend to the maverick pharaoh Akhenaten. In one of
the film's climactic sequences, the pharaoh's followers
are seen worshipping Aten, with the great hymn
echoing around them. The music, scored for a large
choir and full orchestra, was written by legendary
Hollywood composer Alfred Newman, winner of numerous Academy Awards. The marriage of Newman's music and Akhenaten's written words creates
what noted film music critic Jack Smith calls an "exotic, mystical quality." It is "wonderfully ethereal
[heavenly]," he adds, "a profound expression of bliss-
ful, devoted worship." The full score for *The Egyptian*, including Akhenaten's hymn, resurrected in
glory from ancient obscurity, has recently been rere-
corded and remastered on a magnificent CD avail-
able online at Film Score Monthly.

who feeds the son in the womb of his mother,
who quiets him with something to stop his crying;
you are the nurse in the womb,
giving breath to nourish all that has been begotten.
When he comes down from the womb to breathe
on the day he is born,
you open up his mouth completely, and supply his
needs.
When the fledgling in the egg speaks in the shell,
you give him air inside it to sustain him.
When you grant him his allotted time to break out
from the egg,
he comes out from the egg to cry out at his
fulfillment,
and he goes upon his legs when he has come forth
from it.

How plentiful it is, what you have made,
although they are hidden from view,
sole god, without another beside you;
you created the earth as you wished,
when you were by yourself, before
mankind, all cattle and kine,
all beings on land, who fare upon their feet,
and all beings in the air, who fly with their wings.

The lands of Khor [Syria-Palestine] and Kush [Nubia,
south of Egypt]
and the land of Egypt:
you have set every man in his place,
you have allotted their needs,
every one of them according to his diet,
and his lifetime is counted out.
Tongues are separate in speech,
and their characters / as well;
their skins are different,

for you have differentiated the foreigners.
In the underworld you have made a Nile
that you may bring it forth as you wish
to feed the populace,
since you made them for yourself, their utter master,
growing weary on their account, lord of every land.
For them the Aten of the daytime arises,
great in awesomeness.

All distant lands,
you have made them live,
for you have set a Nile in the sky
that it may descend for them
and make waves upon the mountains like the sea
to irrigate the fields in their towns.
How efficient are your designs,
Lord of eternity:
a Nile in the sky for the foreigners
and all creatures that go upon their feet,
a Nile coming back from the underworld for Egypt.

Your rays give suck to every field:
when you rise they live,
and they grow for you.
You have made the seasons
to bring into being all you have made:
the Winter to cool them,
the Heat that you may be felt.

You have made a far-off heaven
in which to rise
in order to observe everything you have made. . . .
When you rise, they live;
when you set, they die.
You are a lifespan in yourself;
one lives by you.

Eyes are / upon your perfection until you set:
all work is put down when you rest in the west.

When (you) rise, (everything) grows
for the King and (for) everyone who hastens on foot,
because you have founded the land
and you have raised them for your son
who has come forth from your body,
the King of Upper and Lower Egypt, the one Living
    on Maat,
Lord of the Two Lands, Nefer-kheperu-Re Wa-en-Re,
son of Re, the one Living on Maat, Master of Regalia,
the long lived,
and the Foremost Wife of the King, whom he loves,
the Mistress of the Two Lands,
Nefer-nefru-Aten Nefertiti [Akhenaten's wife],
living and young, forever and ever.

Akhenaten's Mysterious Physical Attributes

Megaera Lorenz

One of the more striking things about the heretic pharaoh Akhenaten, in addition to his unorthodox religious ideas and policies, was his unusual physical appearance in art. In most of the paintings and sculptures of him that have survived, his body looks deformed in various ways, with abnormally long arms, fingers, and neck, extremely wide hips, and larger-than-normal breasts. A number of explanations have been advanced to explain this mystery, including some that suggest that these attributes were added by the artists for various reasons or, more plausibly, that Akhenaten suffered from some sort of debilitating physical condition, perhaps a rare genetic disorder. In this essay, researcher Megaera Lorenz, who has written extensively about the heretic pharaoh, discusses the main theories for his possible deformity, including the most widely accepted one—that he suffered from Marfan syndrome.

Megaera Lorenz, "The Mystery of Akhenaten: Genetics or Aesthetics?" www. heptune.com, 1996.

While Akhenaten led a reform on the Ancient Egyptian religion, he also revolutionized Egyptian art. He broke the conventions of Egyptian art by showing himself in warm family scenes with his wife and children, and portraying himself and the rest of the royal family in a much more human and naturalistic manner than any of his predecessors had. The most peculiar result of this art reform, however, was the portrayal of the physical characteristics of the pharaoh himself.

In sculptures and paintings of Akhenaten, he is shown as having a long, slender neck, a long face with a sharp chin, narrow, almond-shaped eyes, full lips, long arms and fingers, rounded thighs and buttocks, a soft belly, and enlarged breasts. His odd appearance was particularly prominent in art from the early part of the reign. One early statue portrays the king in the nude and without genitalia of any kind.

These features have puzzled archaeologists since Akhenaten was first discovered in the early nineteenth century, and people have offered many explanations as to why he looked this way.

One of the early theories was that Akhenaten was actually a woman disguised as a man, and was following in Queen Hatshepsut's footsteps, but this idea has been abandoned. The theory that is most in favor at this time is that Akhenaten suffered from some kind of illness or syndrome which caused his odd appearance. The two most likely possibilities proposed in recent years are Froehlich's Syndrome and Marfan's Syndrome. . . .

Froehlich's Syndrome

The most popular belief is that Akhenaten suffered from Froehlich's Syndrome, an endocrine disorder found most commonly in men.

The endocrine system consists of the glands in the

body which produce and release into the bloodstream certain chemicals known as hormones. Hormones regulate various bodily functions, like glucose and insulin levels in the blood, growth, salt metabolism, and sexuality. The main endocrine gland is the pituitary, located in the forebrain. The pituitary gland is divided into two parts: the anterior pituitary, which regulates the activities of the other glands in the system and is also responsible for the release of growth hormone, and the posterior pituitary, which regulates water and salt metabolism. The pituitary is regulated in turn by the hypothalamus, which also regulates hunger and various other biological functions.

Froehlich's Syndrome can be caused by a variety of things, the most common being a tumor in either the pituitary gland or the hypothalamus.

If Froehlich's Syndrome occurs as a tumor only in the pituitary gland, then it mainly seems to affect the secondary sex characteristics in men. The secondary sex characteristics include body hair and deepening of the voice. The reason that Froehlich's Sydrome causes this lack of sexual development is that the gonads or sex glands (the testes, in men) don't function properly as a result of the impaired functioning of the pituitary. Froehlich's Syndrome also results in infertility, a lack of sex drive, and feminine fat distribution.

If Froehlich's Syndrome occurs as a tumor in the hypothalamus, then hunger metabolism is affected, and obesity occurs. Since the hypothalamus regulates the pituitary gland, it then also has the effect of stunting sexual development. Stunted physical growth occurs in either situation. Diabetes can also occur along with Froehlich's Syndrome. Sometimes the pituitary will become overactive and cause an overgrown jaw and skull deformities.

How well does this fit Akhenaten? Overall, not too

well. Some of the characteristics associated with Froehlich's Syndrome seem to fit his apparent peculiarities (such as the feminine figure and the prominent jaw), but many of the main symptoms of the illness do not. Akhenaten, despite the fact that he is shown as a eunuch in some of the artwork from his time, seemed to be quite fertile (we know that he fathered six children, possibly more), did not seem to show stunted physical growth, and was definitely not obese. Another symptom of Froehlich's is severe mental retardation, and it is apparent from literary works by the king that he was not at all retarded. Therefore, it is unlikely that Akhenaten had Froehlich's Syndrome, and historians have turned to another option: Marfan's Syndrome.

Marfan's Syndrome

The most recently suggested possibility for Akhenaten's supposed pathology is a genetic disorder known as Marfan's Syndrome. This is a more likely possibility than Froehlich's Syndrome, as it does not affect intelligence or fertility.

Marfan's Syndrome was first described by a French doctor named Antione B. Marfan, who reported that some of his patients had especially long fingers (he called this arachnodactyly, or spider-fingers), skeletal abnormalities (including arms that were disproportionately long), and high, arched pallets. He also noticed spine defects.

Antione noted that these traits seemed to be inherited, and it is now certain that Marfan's Syndrome is a hereditary disease, and the gene for it is autosomal dominant. A dominant gene is one that will overwrite other genes so that only one is required for the trait that that particular gene carries to be expressed. A person who inherits a dominant gene from one parent will automatically have the trait that the gene produces, unlike with recessive genes in which a gene for the trait must be inherited from each parent for the trait to show. Autosomal means that the gene is on a non-sex chromosome. There are 46 chromosomes in every human cell, and they make 23 pairs, each one connected by a centrome. The 23rd pair consists of the sex chromosomes. The gene for Marfan's Syndrome is located on pair fifteen. This gene causes the occurrence of too many microfibrillar fibers in the connective tissue, which results in a lack of flexibility in the body's tissues. . . .

Skeletal abnormalities that have been noticed in Marfan's patients are a long face, an unusually tall stature, a short upper body in comparison to the lower body (because they have a short ribcage), and overgrown ribs. The latter results in chest deformities such as Pectus Excavatum (funnel chest) or Pectus Carnatum (pigeon breast). A wide pelvis, elongated skull, and prominent shoulder blades are other symptoms. One of the most distinctive characteristics of Marfan's Syndrome is unusually long arms, fingers, and toes. . . .

Because of the excessive fibers in the tissues of people with Marfan's Syndrome, their tissues often stretch to the point of breaking under the strain of normal tissue stress. There are often stretch marks on the skin, as a result of this. When this sort of stretching occurs in the aorta (the major artery that comes out of the heart), it can break, resulting in major complications. Because of the heart problems, people with Marfan's Syndrome usually have a short life-span, perhaps of about thirty years. . . .

From this information, it would seem that Marfan's Syndrome best suits Akhenaten's possible affliction. He did show traits like arachnodactyly, an unusually long face, a tall, slender build, and a wide pelvis. His relatives are shown as having similar features, and elongated skulls. The fact that the rest of his family apparently showed some of these traits also suggests that he had a genetic disorder such as Marfan's Syndrome. He also lived for about the amount of time that a Marfan's victim lives without medical assistance.

Other Theories

Did Akhenaten really have any kind of ailment at all? There is certainly a possibility that there was nothing wrong with him. Any conclusions drawn simply from looking at artwork are highly questionable. If historians three thousand years in the future were to come to the same sorts of conclusions from looking at today's political cartoons, for instance, they would probably think that just about every president or political leader that the U.S. has ever had suffered from some kind of bizarre disorder. A good many people have offered alternative explanations as to why Akhenaten was portrayed so strangely.

One theory is that it was some form of religious symbolism. Because the god Aten was referred to as "The mother and father of all human kind," it has been suggested that Akhenaten was made to look androgynous in artwork as a symbol of the androgyny of the god.

It has also been suggested that the distinctive art of this time was some kind of expressionistic art style, and it has been pointed out that everyone depicted in the artwork of the period showed some of the odd features of the king and his family.

One thing that would suggest that Akhenaten *did* have an illness of some kind was the fact that he remained hidden for a good portion of his father's reign. Normally, a great deal of attention would be devoted to the heir to the throne. It should be noted that Akhenaten had an older brother, Tuthmose, who died at an early age. Perhaps if Marfan's Syndrome did run in the family, Tuthmose's early death was a result of some of the complications associated with the disease. If this were the case, though, one would have to wonder why Tuthmose was not hidden as well. Perhaps he did not show some of the more visible abnormalities that are sometimes present, such as the skeletal problems. The extent to which various symptoms of the illness show up can vary greatly.

Before any specific ailments were suggested, some historians speculated that Akhenaten's possible illness may have somehow accounted for his strange behavior. This is probably not the case, but Akhenaten did call himself "The Unique One of Re," and it would seem that he used his odd appearance as part of this image.

No mummy has yet been identified as being that of Akhenaten. Obviously, it would be hard to tell whether he had symptoms like bad eyesight or heart problems, even if his body *were* to be found. However, the bodies of several of Akhenaten's known relatives have been found, and a reasonably sure way we would have of finding out whether Akhenaten had Marfan's Syndrome would be to do genetic testing on his known relatives. If this were to be done, it would provide invaluable information about Akhenaten and his family.

From Obscurity to Fame: Akhenaten's Ill-Fated Son

Aidan Dodson

The youngest son of Akhenaten, the so-called heretic pharaoh, is known to posterity as Tutankhamen (or Tutankhamun). After the discovery of Tutankhamen's tomb in 1922 by English archaeologist Howard Carter, the world came to call him "King Tut" for short. There is great irony in this young man's life and ultimate legacy. In ways he could not avoid, he was caught up in the social chaos and political infighting surrounding the downfall of his father, whose memory the priests and nobles attempted to discredit and erase. Tutankhamen was a mere boy when he inherited the throne, was overshadowed by powerful, grasping military generals, died young (possibly murdered), and was buried in a secret tomb originally meant for a high official. In the lengthy annals of the Egyptian pharaohs, he was certainly one of the least accomplished and obscure. Yet when Carter unearthed that once secret tomb and revealed its treasures to the modern world, King Tut became and remains the most famous of all ancient Egyptian rulers. This overview of the boy-king's short life and reign (1336–1327 B.C.) is by Egyptologist Aidan Dodson.

Aidan Dodson, *Monarchs of the Nile*. Cairo, Egypt: American University in Cairo Press, 2000. Copyright © 2000 by American University in Cairo Press. Reproduced by permission.

☙ ☙ ☙

Tutankhaten, as he was known when he came to the throne, was almost certainly the younger son of Akhenaten, and once appeared as a prince on a relief, found at Ashmunein and probably originally from Amarna. With the successive deaths of his elder brother and father, the nine- or ten-year-old boy became king, with his sister Ankhesenpaaten as his queen, and the generals Ay and Horemheb as the effective rulers of the country.

Restoring the Religious Status Quo

He seems to have spent the first few years of the reign at Amarna, and probably began a tomb there. However, fairly early on, the royal couple's names were changed to Tutankhamun and Ankhesenamun, and the royal residence shifted back to Memphis, for millennia its traditional location. In his earliest years there, the young king was in the charge of a woman named Maya, whose tomb was recently found at Saqqara. Amarna may have remained for a time as the Aten's ceremonial centre and the royal necropolis, but rapid moves were underway to restore the religious status quo.

The key document in this process is the Restoration Stela, now in Cairo. Extracts will suffice to indicate its import:

> Now when His Person [Tutankamen] had arisen as king, the temples of the gods and goddesses, from Elephantine to the marshes of the Delta . . . had fallen into neglect. Their shrines had fallen into desolation and become overgrown with weeds; their sanctuaries were as if they had never been and their halls were a trodden path. The land was in confusion, the gods having forsaken it. If an army was sent to Syria to widen the frontiers of Egypt, it met with

no success. If one prayed to a god to ask things of him, he did not come. . . .

After some time had passed thus, His Person appeared on the throne of his father. . . . See, His Person was in his palace in the estate of Tuthmosis I . . . and took council of his heart, searching out every effective occasion, seeking what was beneficial to his father Amun, for fashioning his august image of real electrum. He has added to what was done in former times, he has fashioned an image of his father Amun upon thirteen carrying-poles, his holy image being of electrum, lapis-lazuli, turquoise and every rare costly stone. . . .

The text continues, listing the king's numerous benefactions to the gods, thus establishing Tutankhamun as the restorer of the sanctuaries abandoned during Akhenaten's reign. Certainly there are many temple-statues attributable to Tutankhamun's reign, his tenure on the throne being distinguished by a particularly delicate artistic style that combines all the best features of Amarna and traditional work.

Construction Projects and Military Campaigns

Amongst his Theban works were the continuance of the entrance colonnade of Amenophis III's temple at Luxor, complete with associated statues. Karnak was embellished with three-dimensional images of Amun, Amunet and Khonsu, not to mention a whole range of statues and sphinxes depicting the king himself, and a small temple in the king's name. Various fragments at Memphis attest to his buildings there, while at Faras, in Nubia, he was worshipped as a god during his lifetime. Also in the far south, he built a temple at Kawa, from which ultimately came the magnificent pair of granite lions that today flank the entrance to the Egyptian

Sculpture Gallery at the British Museum. Finally, his reign apparently saw the first interment of an Apis bull, the bovine incarnation of the god Ptah, at Saqqara, accompanied by some particularly fine canopic jars and three glass pendants, naming the king.

Nubia was ruled by the Viceroy Huy, well-known from his fine tomb at Thebes. Other high officials were the viziers Usermontju and Pentu, but the most influential were clearly the already mentioned military men, Ay and Horemheb. The former was the probable brother of Tiye and father of Nefertiti, the latter a man of provincial stock who was commander of the army and king's deputy. The treasurer Maya was also a prominent figure, as was Ay's likely son, the General Nakhtmin. Both Maya and Nakhtmin were to present gifts at the king's funeral, while both the former and Horemheb built magnificent tombs at Saqqara. The superb reliefs in Horemheb's tomb include indications of the military expeditions that Horemheb undertook to prove that the blight on campaigning referred to in the Restoration Stela had been removed by Tutankhamun's generous gifts to the gods.

These campaigns were aimed at reasserting Egypt's position amongst her vassals and dependants; they included operations against Libyans, Nubians and Asiatics, the depictions of the prisoners in the tomb of Horemheb providing amazingly accurately studied images of human beings under duress. The reliefs include the victorious Horemheb's reward before Tutankhamun and Ankhesenamun: only a few years later, the general would be king, and shown in the tombs of his followers rewarding them in exactly the same way.

The Boy-King's Tomb
Like all Egyptian kings, Tutankhamun will, in spite of his tender years, have given thought to his tomb. It is known that the Amarna necropolis workmen remained

in place for some time into his reign, and it seems very likely that for a number of years it was intended that he be buried there. His planned resting place was most probably a tomb now numbered 29 in the Amarna series, which had reached some forty-five metres into the bedrock before being abandoned. The sarcophagus that had been intended to hold the king's remains had originally been intended to follow Akhenaten's in design, with the queen's figure on the corners instead of the traditional protective goddesses of burial. After the king's abandonment of Atenism, the great quartzite box was extensively reworked to give his new name, and to convert the figures on its corners to the time-hallowed Isis, Nephthys, Neith and Selqet.

Tut's Untimely Death

When the decision was made to move the royal tomb-site to Thebes, work must have begun on a new sepulchre in the Valley of the Kings. Regrettably, it is uncertain as to which tomb this was, since it was never finished. . . . The tomb was left unfinished because, after little more than nine years on the throne, and probably not yet out of his teens, Tutankhamun died. In spite of much speculation, and a number of examinations, no certain conclusions have been reached as to the cause of death, though it is possible that a blow to the head was involved. His two daughters having both been still-born, the male line of the Eighteenth Dynasty died with him.

A tomb in the Valley of the Kings, intended for a very high official (Ay?), was appropriated for the king's burial, and after a modest extension received his mummy and funerary equipment. The latter included a number of items, including a coffin and the canopic coffinettes, that had been long ago made for Neferneferuaten, but discarded by Akhenaten.

After a ritual meal, the debris of which, together with the refuse from the king's embalming, was placed just inside the tomb's entrance, the latter was sealed and, apart from two minor intrusions, was to remain closed until 1922, when Howard Carter's excavations revealed the tomb and its treasures to the world.

Profiles · in · History

Ramesses II and the Battle of Kadesh

Ramesses Wages War and Negotiates Peace

Mark Healy

Next to Thutmose III, Ramesses (or Ramasses) II was the most illustrious warrior pharaoh of the New Kingdom. Much of the energy Ramesses expended during his reign was devoted to preparations for and execution of military campaigns, especially in the area of Syria-Palestine, the strategic corridor that connected Egypt to rival kingdoms in other parts of the Near East. Among others, these included Mitanni (centered in what is now western Iraq), and Hatti, land of the Hittites (in what is now Turkey), which eventually contributed to Mitanni's decline. The climax of Ramesses' military endeavors was the great battle of Kadesh (or Qadesh, in what is now southern Syria), in which he clashed with the Hittites and kept them from overrunning Palestine. Ramesses could also be an effective diplomat and peacemaker, as evidenced by the sophisticated treaty he eventually signed with the Hittite king. This informative overview of these important events is by Mark Healy, a noted scholar of ancient Egyptian military affairs.

❦ ❦ ❦

Ramasses II was about 25 years of age when he ascended the throne of Egypt in 1304 B.C., absolute master of one of the world's great powers. He was young, vigorous, able and resourceful; but above all, full of ambition to emulate his illustrious forebears of the early 18th Dynasty by extending Egypt's northern frontiers to encompass again the territories of central Syria, notwithstanding that those territories lay firmly within the Hittite sphere and that such was tacitly recognised by the treaty agreed with Hatti by his father Seti I. Fulfilment of his ambition meant that Ramasses accepted the inevitability of war with Egypt's powerful northern rival. Although he was unable to engage in military operations in Syria until Year Four of his reign, it is apparent that from an early date much energy was expended within Egypt in preparing the army for its coming contest with Hatti. This included adding a fourth field army to the order of battle, and the expansion of the eastern Delta city of Pi-Ramasses to act as the forward supply base for Egyptian operations in the Levant.

Ramasses' First Campaign
In the spring of 1301 B.C. Ramasses led his army northwards to the Levant [Syria-Palestine] for first time. Their passage along the Phoenician coast is traceable by the inscriptions he left at the ports of Tyre and Byblos. Reaching as far as Simyra, Ramasses then turned inland and attacked the kingdom of Amurru, a known vassal of the Hittites. With the Egyptian army at his gates and the Hittite army too far distant to offer support, Benteshina, the ruler of Amurru, had little choice but to inform [the Hittite king] Muwatallish that it was Ramasses II he now acknowledged as his suzerain [overlord]. The pharaoh had now created the conditions for a future attack on Qadesh from two directions, one

from the south through the Bekaa Valley and the other from Amurru itself. Both would be employed in the following year. The campaign complete, Ramasses and the army returned to Egypt with the young pharaoh greatly optimistic about the likelihood of regaining the 'lost' territories of central Syria in the following year.

Qadesh's Strategic Location

There is no doubt that Muwatallish saw the Egyptian campaign as the first stage of a concerted attempt to recover their position in central Syria and thereafter extend their power into the north of the region. Unwilling to stand passively by and see the whole Hittite position in Syria demolished, Muwatallish resolved upon a strategy that would put [a stop] to any further Egyptian aspirations in the region. The military campaign now planned for the following year identified two major tasks. Amurru was to be recovered; and the Egyptian army given such a trouncing that Ramasses would be denied the means to realise any of his wider political and territorial ambitions in the region.

It was clear many months before the battle took place that Qadesh would be the arena of contest. The Egyptians had contended ownership of the city with Mitanni and then Hatti since the days of Tuthmosis III. Such consistent and prolonged interest in the site arose naturally from its strategic position: not only was it the key to the Eleutheros Plain and therefore to Amurru, it was also the door to the Syrian Plain, and must be central to Ramasses' aspirations to extend Egyptian rule into northern Syria. . . .

The site gave immense advantage to the Hittites. Muwatallish was operating in territory under Hittite control, supplied by loyal vassals and at the end of relatively short lines of communication, whereas the Egyptians would be operating some 1,600km from their home base. Furthermore, the city itself was large enough to accommodate the Hittite army should the battle go against them. It was also a very strongly fortified position, being enclosed by a moat and surrounded by the River Orontes itself.

The army organised by the Hittite king was one of the largest ever assembled by the kingdom of Hatti. However, no document has come to light from that source detailing either its make-up or strength. All speculation concerning such matters must rest solely upon the details provided by the various Egyptian accounts of the Qadesh campaign. . . .

Ramasses speaks of the Hittites and their 18 allied and vassal states fielding as many as 3,700 chariots and 37,000 foot soldiers.

The Pharaoh's Army on the March

Throughout the months of March and April the city of Pi-Ramasses became the assembly point for one of the largest armies ever raised by the Egyptians. Units were allocated to one of the four field armies (also referred to in the text as divisions). Noticeable was the increasing use of foreign troops in the regular army; indeed this was to become even more marked in the centuries ahead. Apart from the Nubians and Sherden, Libyans and Canaanites were now in the employ of the standing army as mercenaries. The Egyptian character of the army was being diluted not just to increase manpower but also in pursuit of a deliberate policy to diversify the ethnic basis of the army as much as possible. The total strength of the Egyptian force was in the region of 20,000 men divided equally among the four field armies. Chariot strength is not given as a separate figure, but by this date the Egyptians must have been able to muster a very significant force.

Leaving Egypt at the end of April, the army took the coast road to Gaza, where Ramasses divided his forces.

Turning inland with the bulk of his army, he followed the route through Canaan, traversing the eastern side of Lake Galilee and marching via the southern end of the Anti-Lebanon range and entering the Bekaa Valley to reach Kumidi. The smaller of the two forces, clearly an élite unit and one which was to play a decisive role in the battle, had been detached to advance northwards from Gaza along the coast road to Phoenicia. Their task was to ensure the loyalty of the Phoenician coastal cities by a show of force. However, their line of march from the coast was inland to bring them to Qadesh via the Eleutheros Valley in Amurru. The pharaoh had no doubt impressed on their commander the need to arrive on a specific date, and therein lay their importance to Ramasses' strategy. It is clear when examining subsequent events that the Hittites were unaware of this detached unit.

Identified in the Qadesh inscriptions as simply the 'Ne'arin', the question needs to be asked who exactly they were. The term itself means 'young men' and suggests that they were a crack Canaanite unit serving in the standing army and whose loyalty to Ramasses II was beyond question. It is most likely that they were *mariyannu* [young warriors] equipped as a well-armed flying column with chariots, chariot runners and other supporting infantry, able to traverse the greater distance to Qadesh and still reach the vicinity of the city on the appointed day. It is, however, of some interest that some commentators have suggested this unit was in fact the fourth army division named for Set.

Ramasses' Miscalculation

Exactly one month after leaving Egypt Ramasses was encamped with the division of Amun on the morning of day 9 of the third month of Shemu (late May) on the Kamu'at el-Harmel ridge to the south of Qadesh. From this vantage point the valley lay ahead with the city it-

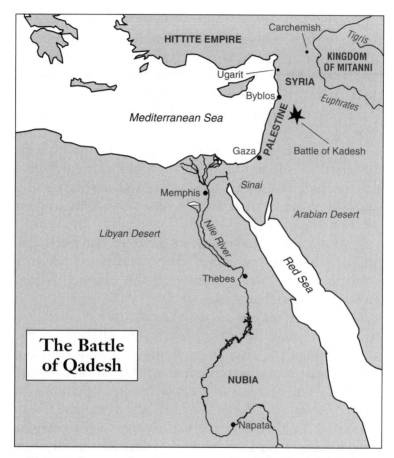

The Battle of Qadesh

self in sight. At this point the other field armies—Re, Ptah and Set—lay to the rear of Amun along the line of march and separated by about one *iter* (about 10.5km), according to standard operating procedure. Striking camp, Ramasses and Amun descended from the ridge, traversed the forest of Labwi and began crossing the Orontes by the ford at Shabtuna. It was then that two Shasu-bedouin (whom it is generally assumed had been deliberately sent out by the Hittite king to misinform Ramasses) appeared and offered the information that Muwatallish and his army were nowhere near Qadesh, but in the land of Aleppo to the north of the city of Tunip, some 120 miles distant. If true, this would place Ramasses in a very strong position: he could collect his army, ensure that it was rested, and be ready for battle before the Hittites arrived. In short, he could do to them exactly what they intended to do to him.

Subsequent events can only be understood if we accept that Ramasses, through gullibility deriving from blind optimism and over-confidence, accepted this information without question. It would certainly seem that no reconnaissance was ordered as verification. If such was the case, then the outcome was a matter of absolute negligence. . . .

It seems that if such a reconnaissance had been carried out then the presence of Muwatallish and his large army in such close proximity to the east of Qadesh must have been detected.

As it was, Ramasses advanced forthwith. With the division of Amun he established camp slightly to the north-west of the city, in ignorance of the presence of the Hittites carefully screened on the far side of the Orontes. The division of Re was by now beginning to cross the Shabtuna ford. While scouts might have been noticeable by their absence earlier, their activities now gave Ramasses his first intimation that all was far from well. Muwatallish, having received information that Ramasses was advancing on Qadesh from, in all likelihood, the very Shasu-bedouin who had misled Ramasses, despatched his own scouts to locate the pharaoh's exact position. It was two of these scouts whom their Egyptian counterparts now captured. Beaten, they were dragged in front of the pharaoh:

'Then said His Majesty, "What are you?" They replied, "We belong to the ruler of Hatti! He sent us out to see where Your Majesty was." Said His Majesty to them, "Where is he, the Ruler of Hatti? See, I heard it said that he was in the land of Aleppo, north of Tunip." They replied, "Behold, the Ruler of Hatti has already come, together with many foreign lands that he brought as allies. . . . See, they are poised armed and ready to fight behind Old Qadesh?'"

Attack and Counterattack

The reaction of the incredulous pharaoh was to call an immediate conference with his senior officers, the outcome of which was the dispatch, post haste, of the vizier southwards to demand the rapid concentration of the divisions of Ptah and Set on Qadesh. Until their arrival Ramasses must depend on the power of the divisions of Amun and Re to resist any immediate Hittite attack. In this he was to be disappointed. As Re marched across the plain towards the camp of Amun, Muwatallish launched a major attack against the flank of the extended, marching division.

Emerging from dead ground and cover, a mighty host of Hittite chariotry poured across the Orontes to the immediate south of Qadesh itself and crashed into the flank of Re. The protective screen of Egyptian chariots was simply swept away by the sheer weight of the Hittite charge. While the exact size of the Hittite force is still a matter of great dispute, it is clear that it was sufficiently large to overwhelm the division of Re; however, it could not have approached in any way the vast figure of 2,500 chariots implied by Ramasses and seemingly quoted in such an uncritical fashion by so many commentators. The notion that a large Hittite detachment rather than the full chariot force was involved renders their rapid transit across the Orontes ford quite credible. It also places the 'single-handed' opposition of Ramasses later in the proceedings within the bounds of credibility as well.

With their own protective chariotry vanquished the cohesion of the Egyptian infantry companies—who were totally unprepared for combat—evaporated, and blind panic led to the disintegration of the whole of the division, with the survivors fleeing northwards towards the camp of Amun. From the vantage point of the camp of Amun the scene that now unfolded must have been desperate to behold. Behind the lines of fleeing infantry trying to reach the shield wall of Amun, huge numbers of Hittite chariots could be seen hurtling towards the camp, raising a wall of dust, their thousands of horses' hooves pounding the hard earth like thunder. Countless Egyptian infantry were ridden down or speared from behind by the chariot crews. The wave of panic then engulfed the camp of Amun, the defenders abandoning their positions and weapons as the Hittite chariotry broke in from the western side.

Watching the calamity from his own camp, which was set apart from that of Amun, Ramasses acted in perhaps the only way open to him if the rout was to be prevented from degenerating into a disaster. Donning his battle-armour, he mounted his chariot and prepared to go into action against the Hittite chariots virtually single-handed. Moving towards the enemy at speed, while at the same time appealing to his fleeing troops to rally, the pharaoh attacked the enemy with the assistance of perhaps only his immediate chariot-borne entourage. Launching themselves at the Hittite eastern flank, the small numbers of Egyptian chariots proceeded to wreak havoc among the enemy, whose own cohesion and momentum was rapidly dissipating.

Utilising to the full the remarkable speed and manoeuvrability of the Egyptian chariots, Ramasses and his few supporters began to pick off the enemy in large numbers. With a ferocity born of desperation the pharaoh and his supporters attacked, turned and attacked again at least six times. In the swirling mêlée it is very possible that the Hittites were not aware of the small size of the force attacking them. From a vantage point overlooking the camp of Amun from across the river, Muwatallish could see how Ramasses was beginning to rectify the situation; and ordered a second wave of chariots across the river to support the first wave, who were now in trouble.

Reinforcements Arrive

Once again we are faced with the problem of numbers. It is unlikely that the Hittite second wave contained as many as 1,000 chariots. Reaction time for Muwatallish was critical—he had to get chariots across the Orontes to attack Ramasses at once. He used those he had to hand, which in all likelihood meant the aristocratic entourage who surrounded his person and who were sharing his view of the pharaoh's counterattack. They crossed the Orontes, but instead of making for Ramasses headed instead for his camp in the hope of distracting him from his harrying of the first group of Hittite chariots. However, the appearance on the scene at this moment of the *Ne'arin* prevented this. They attacked the Hittite reinforcements, and were later joined by Ramasses. In the subsequent contest few of the second wave of Hittite chariotry escaped back across the river, and many of those slain were of high rank from among the Hittite and allied states serving Muwatallish.

By the end of the day the pharaoh had managed to recoup the situation. The division of Amun was reassembled, and that of Ptah had also arrived at Qadesh by a forced march. In the aftermath of the battle it would seem that Ramasses may have visited grim punishment on many of his troops in the divisions of Amun and Re, who in his eyes had committed treason against his person by running away. According to some scholars there is evidence that on the day following the battle he ordered a decimation [execution of several soldiers chosen at random from the ranks] among his troops in full view of the Hittite king.

An offer from the Hittite king of a military disen-
gagement on the basis of peaceful co-existence was
accepted by the pharaoh. While no hard and fast territorial demarcation followed, Ramasses never again cam-
paigned in recognisably Hittite territory. Although he
was engaged in Amurru some three years after Qadesh
this was clearly not seen as a provocation by the Hittites,
who by now had more immediate problems to face in
the rise of Assyria on their eastern frontier and those
territories to the north of Hatti.

It was in Year Twenty-One of Ramasses' reign that a
formal treaty of peace was signed between Egypt and
Hatti. Sealed by the marriage of the daughter of the
Hittite king to Ramasses II, the treaty encompassed
both a mutual defence pact and a formal demarcation of
their respective territories in Syria. Whilst Ramasses
was never to emulate Tuthmosis III, he inaugurated a
treaty with the kingdom of Hatti that would be upheld
by both powers until the great northern empire was
swept away in the tide of human migration that covered
the Near East at the beginning of the 12th century B.C.
By then, however, Ramasses II had already been in his
grave for nearly 50 years.

Ramesses' Kadesh Inscriptions

Scribes of Ramesses II

The Egyptians fought hundreds of battles in dozens of campaigns stretching over the long years of the Old, Middle, and New Kingdoms. Yet only one battle, perhaps the greatest and most strategic of all, was recorded in any detail—the one fought at Kadesh (or Qadesh), in Syria, circa 1274 B.C., between Ramesses II and his army and a large army of Hittites. It was not only the only Egyptian battle, but also the earliest battle in world history for which a specific play-by-play account can be reconstructed. This is thanks to the survival of a series of relief sculptures accompanied by inscriptions at Ramesses' mortuary temple at Thebes. Supplementing this so-called "Official Record" is another source, referred to as "Poem," probably written by one of Ramesses' scribes. The "Official Record" and "Poem," both of which are excerpted here (from J.H. Breasted's translation), are similar in some ways; however, each covers a few aspects of the battle the other does not. For example, the "Official Record" includes an account of Ramesses' encounter with two Hittite spies sent to trick the pharaoh into falling into an ambush. (Note that the epithet "the vanquished chief of Kheta," which appears throughout both accounts, is the Hittite king, Muwatallis; it was the custom of the Egyptians to hold their enemies in contempt in written accounts.)

Scribes of Ramesses II, "The Asiatic War," *Ancient Records of Egypt, Volume 3: The Nineteenth Dynasty*, edited and translated by J.H. Breasted. New York: Russell and Russell, 1962.

🐝 🐝 🐝

The Poem

His majesty proceeded northward, and he then arrived at the highland of Kadesh. Then his majesty marched before, like his father, Montu lord of Thebes, and crossed over the channel of the Orontes, there being with him the first division of Amon. . . .

When his majesty reached the city [of Kadesh] behold, the wretched, vanquished chief of Kheta had come, having gathered together all countries from the ends of the sea to the land of Kheta. . . . He left not a country which was not brought, together with their chiefs who were with him, every man bringing his chariotry, an exceeding great multitude, without its like. They covered the mountains and the valleys; they were like grasshoppers with their multitudes. . . .

Behold, the wretched, vanquished chief of Kheta, together with the numerous allied countries, were stationed in battle array, concealed on the northwest of the city of Kadesh, while his majesty was alone by himself, [with] his bodyguard, and the division of Amon was marching behind him. The division of Re crossed over the river-bed on the south side of the town of Shabtuna at the distance of an iter [about 1⅓ miles] from the division of Amon. The division of Ptah was on the south of the city of Aranami and the division of Sutekh was marching upon the road. . . . Behold, the wretched vanquished chief of Kheta was stationed in the midst of the infantry which was with him, and he came not out to fight, for fear of his majesty. Then he made to go the people of the chariotry, an exceedingly numerous multitude like the sand, being three people to each span. Now, they had made their combinations (thus): among every three youths was one man of the vanquished of Kheta, equipped with all the weapons of battle. Lo, they had stationed them in battle array, concealed on the northwest the city of Kadesh.

They came forth from the southern side of Kadesh, and they cut through the division of Re in its middle, while they were marching without knowing and without being drawn up for battle. The infantry and chariotry of his majesty retreated before them. Now, his majesty had halted on the north of the city of Kadesh, on the western side of the Orontes. Then came one [a messenger] to tell it to his majesty.

His majesty shone like his father Montu, when he took the adornments of war; as he seized his coat of mail, he was like Baal in his hour. . . . His majesty halted in the rout, then he charged into the foe, the vanquished of Kheta, being alone by himself and none other with him. When his majesty went to look behind him, he found 2,500 chariotry surrounding him, in his way out, being all the youth of the wretched Kheta, together with its numerous allied countries. . . .

The Official Record
The tent of his majesty was on the highland south of Kadesh.

When his majesty appeared like the rising of Re, he assumed the adornments of his father, Montu. When the king proceeded northward, and his majesty had arrived at the locality south of the town of Shabtuna, there came two Shasu [enemy soldiers] to speak to his majesty as follows: "Our brethren, who belong to the greatest of the families with the vanquished chief of Kheta, have made us come to his majesty, to say: 'We will be subjects of Pharaoh and we will flee from the vanquished chief of Kheta; for the vanquished chief of

Was Ramesses II the Pharaoh of Oppression?

Over the years, a number of scholars, as well as many non-scholars, have taken for granted the idea that Ramesses II oppressed the Israelites, as told in the Old Testament. Other scholars disagree, including archaeologist David M. Rohl, who argues here that the oppression, if a real event, occurred considerably earlier than Ramesses' time.

The inscriptions on the monuments of Egypt brought one pharaoh to the fore above all others. The names, titles and deeds of Ramesses II were everywhere—on monuments bigger and more imposing than anything belonging to his predecessors or successors (excluding, of course, the mighty pyramids of Giza). The nineteenth century world called him 'Ramesses the Great' in recognition of his spectacular accomplishments. This powerful and long-lived 19th Dynasty pharaoh built many cities and temples in the delta but, most significantly, he founded a new capital in the region which he named Pi-Ramesse—'the estate of Ramesses'. . . .

According to I Kings 6:1–2, the Exodus from Egypt took place four hundred and eighty years before the construction of the First Temple of Jerusalem. The building of the First Temple dedicated to Yahweh was begun in the fourth regnal year of King Solomon. . . . This places the Exodus—according to the biblical data—securely in the fifteenth century B.C. (*c.* 1447 B.C. using modern calculations). Now Egyptologists had already worked out, by the middle of the last century, that Ramesses II's sixty-seven year reign had fallen within the thirteenth century B.C. (the modern preferred dates are 1279–1213 B.C.). Clearly then there is a two-century discrepancy between the biblical date for the building of the store-city of Raamses and the Egyptological date for the building of Pi-Ramesse. Furthermore, even if it could be argued that Ramesses II redly was the Pharaoh of the Oppression (and Exodus) and the Israelites did indeed build his new capital of Pi-Ramesse, we would then not expect to find earlier references in the Old Testament to a location called 'Raamses'; nor were there any pharaohs called Ramesses before Ramesses II's grandfather, Ramesses I (c. 1295 B.C.). The royal name Ramesses is a 19th Dynasty phenomenon. No such placename existed before that time. Egyptian royal cities were named after their royal founders. So Raamses was built by Ramesses. But Genesis 47:11 clearly states that when Joseph had become vizier of Egypt he 'settled his father (Jacob) and brothers, giving them land holdings in Egypt, in the best part of the country—the region of Ramesses—as Pharaoh had ordered'. So the Israelites settled in the 'region of Ramesses' centuries before the first king called Ramesses ascended the throne in Egypt! . . . So why should we so readily accept that Ramesses II was the Pharaoh of the Oppression simply because, according to the book of Exodus, the Israelites built the store-city of Raamses? It is quite possible . . . that the Israelites built an earlier city at the same spot which, by the sixth century B.C., was hidden deep under the ruins of Pi-Ramesse. The biblical redactor would naturally refer to the city by the name which was familiar to all his contemporaries—and that name was 'Ramesses' (this part of the delta was still referred to as Ramesses even as late as the fourth century A.D.).

David M. Rohl, *Pharaohs and Kings: A Biblical Quest.* New York: Crown, 1995, pp. 114–16.

Kheta sits in the land of Aleppo, on the north of Tunip. He fears [the armed might] of Pharaoh [and refuses] to come southward.'" Now, these Shasu spake these words, which they spake to his majesty, falsely, (for) the vanquished chief of Kheta made them come to spy where his majesty was, in order to cause the army of his majesty not to draw up for fighting him. . . .

Lo, the vanquished chief of Kheta came with every chief of every country, their infantry and their chariotry, which he had brought with him by force, and stood, equipped, drawn up in line of battle behind Kadesh the Deceitful, while his majesty knew it not. Then his majesty proceeded northward and arrived on the northwest of Kadesh; and the army of his majesty made camp there.

Then, as his majesty sat upon a throne of gold, there arrived a scout who was in the following of his majesty, and he brought two scouts of the vanquished chief of Kheta. They were conducted into the presence, and his majesty said to them: "What are ye?" They said: "As for us, the vanquished chief of the Kheta has caused that we should come to spy out where his majesty is." Said his majesty to them: "He! Where is he, the vanquished chief of Kheta? Behold, I have heard, saying: 'He is in the land of Aleppo.'" Said they: "See, the vanquished chief of Kheta is stationed, together with many countries, which has brought with him by force. . . . More numerous are they than the sand of the shore. See, they are standing, drawn up for battle, behind Kadesh the Deceitful.". . .

Lo, while his majesty sat talking, . . . the vanquished chief of Kheta came, and the numerous countries, which were with him. They crossed over the channel on the south of Kadesh, and charged into the army of his majesty while they were marching, and not expecting it. Then the infantry and chariotry of his majesty retreated before them, northward to the place where his majesty was. Lo, the foes of the vanquished chief of Kheta surrounded the bodyguard of his majesty, who were by his side.

When his majesty saw them, he was enraged against them, like his father, Montu, lord of Thebes. He seized the adornments of battle, and arrayed himself in his coat of mail. He was like Baal in his hour. Then he betook himself to his horses, and led quickly on, being alone by himself. He charged into the foes of the vanquished chief of Kheta, and the numerous countries which were with him. His majesty was . . . great in strength, smiting and slaying among them; his majesty hurled them headlong, one upon another into the water of the Orontes.

"I charged all countries, while I was alone, my infantry and my chariotry having forsaken me. Not one among them stood to turn about. I swear, as Re loves me, as my father, Atum, favors me, that, as for every matter which his majesty has stated, I did it in truth, in the presence of my infantry and my chariotry."

Treaty Between Ramesses and the Hittite King

Egyptian and Hittite Negotiators

The battle fought at Kadesh about 1274 B.C. was largely indecisive. After Ramesses and the Hittite king, Muwatallis, reluctantly agreed to a temporary peace, each returned to his country and claimed victory, despite the fact that there was no clear winner. Nearly a generation of uneasy standoff ensued until about 1259 B.C., when Ramesses signed a treaty with a new Hittite king, Hattusilis III. The surviving document contains provisions calling for both sides to refrain from further aggression, to help each other against attack by a third party, and to turn over to each other any political fugitives that might flee from one country to the other. This translation of the treaty, which affords a glimpse of the diplomacy and statesmanship of one of the greater pharaohs, is by noted scholar A.H. Gardiner.

🍂 🍂 🍂

Copy of the tablet of silver which the great chief of Hatti, Hattusilis, caused to be brought to Pharaoh by

S. Langdon and A.H. Gardiner, "The Treaty of Alliance Between Hattusilis, King of the Hittites, and the Pharaoh Rameses II of Egypt," translated by A.H. Gardiner, *Journal of Egyptian Archaeology*, vol. 6, 1920, pp. 58–60.

the hand of his messenger Tartesub and his messenger Ramose, in order to beg peace from the Majesty of Usi-ma-Re-setpen-Re, son of Re, Ramesse-mi-Amun [Ramses II], bull of rulers, who makes his boundary where he will in every land. . . .

Peace and Brotherhood

Behold, Hattusilis, the great chief of Hatti, has made himself in a treaty with [Ramses], the great ruler of Egypt, beginning with this day, to cause to be made good peace and good brotherhood between us forever; and he is in brotherhood with me and at peace with me, and I am in brotherhood with him and at peace with him forever.

And since Muwattallis, the great chief of Hatti, my brother, hastened after his fate, and Hattusilis took his seat as great chief of Hatti on the throne of his father; behold I have become with Ramesse-mi-Amun, the great ruler of Egypt, we being together in our peace and our brotherhood; and it is better than the peace and the brotherhood of formerly, which was in the land.

Behold I, being the great chief of Hatti, am with Ramesse-mi-Amun, the great ruler of Egypt, in good peace and good brotherhood.

And the children of the children of the great chief of Hatti shall be in brotherhood and at peace with the children of the children of Ramesse-mi-Amun, the great ruler of Egypt; they being in our policy of brotherhood and our policy of peace.

And the land of Egypt with the land Hatti shall be at peace and in brotherhood like us forever; and hostilities shall not be made between them forever.

Mutual Nonaggression

And the great chief of Hatti shall not trespass into the land of Egypt forever to take aught from it; and [Ramses], the great ruler of Egypt, shall not trespass into the land of Hatti to take aught from it forever. . . .

Mutual Defense

And if another enemy come to the lands of [Ramses], the great ruler of Egypt and he send to the great chief of Hatti saying, "Come with me as help against him"; the great chief of Hatti shall come to him, the great chief of Hatti shall slay his enemy.

But if it be not the desire of the great chief of Hatti to come, he shall send his troops and his chariotry and shall slay his enemy.

Or if Ramesse-mi-Amun, the great ruler of Egypt, become incensed against servants of his, and they do another offense against him, and he go to slay his enemy; the great chief of Hatti shall act with him to destroy everyone against whom they shall be incensed.

Extradition of Fugitives

If any great man flee from the land of Egypt and he come to the lands of the great chief of Hatti; or a town or a district . . . belonging to the lands of Ramesse-mi-Amun, the great ruler of Egypt, and they come to the great chief of Hatti: the great chief of Hatti shall not receive them. The great chief of Hatti shall cause them to be brought to [Ramses], the great ruler of Egypt, their lord, on account of it.

Or if one [common] man or two men who are unknown flee . . . and they come to the land of Hatti, they shall be brought to Ramesse-mi-Amun, the great ruler of Egypt.

Immunity of Fugitives

If one man flee from the land of Egypt, or two, or three, and they come to the great chief of Hatti, the great chief of Hatti shall seize them and shall cause them to be brought back to [Ramses], the great ruler of Egypt. But as for the man who shall be brought to Ramesse-mi-Amun, the great ruler of Egypt, let not his crime be charged against him, let not his house, his wives or his children be destroyed, let him not be killed, let no injury be done to his eyes, to his ears, to his mouth or to his legs, let not any crime be charged against him.

Divine Witnesses

As for these words of the treaty made by the great chief of Hatti with Ramesse-mi-Amun, the great ruler of Egypt, in writing upon this tablet of silver; as for these words, a thousand gods, male gods and female gods of those of the land of Hatti, together with a thousand gods, male gods and female gods of those of the land of Egypt—they are with me as witnesses hearing these words. . . .

As to these words which are upon this tablet of silver of the land of Hatti and of the land of Egypt, as to him who shall not keep them, a thousand gods of the land of Hatti and a thousand gods of the land of Egypt shall destroy his house, his land and his servants. But he who shall keep these words which are on this tablet of silver, be they Hatti, or be they Egyptians, and who do not neglect them, a thousand gods of the land of Hatti and a thousand gods of the land of Egypt will cause him to be healthy and to live, together with his houses and his land and his servants.

Profiles . in . History

Cleopatra: Egypt's Last Pharaoh

Cleopatra's Royal House: The Ptolemaic Rulers

Michael Grant

Egypt's last gasp of independence as a nation came under a dynasty of foreign-born rulers, the last of whom was the famous Queen Cleopatra. One of Alexander the Great's most powerful successors, Ptolemy, seized control of Egypt in the late fourth century B.C. and took the title of Ptolemy I Soter (Savior). Along with the Greek Seleucid and Macedonian kingdoms (lying northeast and north of Egypt), Ptolemaic Egypt was what modern historians call a Hellenistic ("Greek-like") realm, because it consisted of a local Near Eastern culture overlaid with a veneer of supposedly superior Greek culture that had been imposed by the Greek rulers and nobles. This absorbing overview of the rise and fall of the Ptolemies and life in Egypt under their administration is by Michael Grant, a noted historian and author of numerous studies of ancient Greece and Rome.

☙ ☙ ☙

Michael Grant, *From Alexander to Cleopatra: The Hellenistic World*. New York: Charles Scribner's Sons, 1982. Copyright © 1982 by Michael Grant Publications, Ltd. Reproduced by permission of the publisher.

Uniquely shaped by the narrow but immensely fertile Nile valley, Egypt possessed formidable potential resources and strength: and Greeks had always been well aware of this. During the two centuries before Alexander, the country had been under the domination of the Achaemenid Persian empire, whose ruler Cambyses had invaded the country in 525 and dethroned the Egyptian Pharaoh. A native revolt in *c.* 410–404 was successful, but Artaxerxes III Ochus re-established Persian authority in 341. Nine years later, however, Alexander the Great occupied the whole of Egyptian territory without opposition, its population welcoming him as a liberator.

The Rapid Rise of Alexandria

He left the ancient Egyptian city of Memphis as the capital of the country, but immediately set about the foundation of a new Greek colony at Alexandria. It was a mark of genius to see in the meagre fishing village of Rhacotis the immense and spectacular city of the future. Whereas most of Alexander's colonies were located and planned for a military purpose, it is probable that he founded Alexandria for commercial reasons, to take the place of Tyre in Phoenicia, which he had destroyed.

Alexandria faced both ways, and was defensible from either side: it was linked to the interior of the country by Nile canals debouching in Lake Mareotis, and to the north it had two fine harbours opening on to the Mediterranean. With the Pharos lighthouse planned by Sostratus of Cnidus under Ptolemy I Soter, and completed under his son Ptolemy II Philadelphus (*c.* 279), as their symbol and unfailing guide (it ranked as one of the Seven Wonders of the World), these harbours were fully able to accommodate the large ships of the epoch. Alexandria made one set of fortunes by exporting the surpluses of Egypt, and another by its maritime trading all over the near and middle east. With dazzling speed it became the largest of all Greek cities. Dominated by a principal avenue of unprecedented width, it extended over a rectangular area measuring four miles by three-quarters of a mile, and contained, before the end of the third century, something like half a million inhabitants. These included the largest Greek (and partly Macedonian) population of any colonial foundation; the place persistently maintained its Greek customs—and for a long time preserved sentimental ties with the city-states of the homeland. The Greeks of Alexandria had their own exceptional privileges and organization (*politeuma*), but no assembly and probably no council (or had one at first, but soon lost it). The large Jewish community, too, possessed an autonomous *politeuma* of its own. But in addition, outside any civic organization, Alexandria housed tens of thousands of Egyptians and people of innumerable other races. For it was an immensely cosmopolitan centre, the first and greatest universal city, the supreme Hellenistic melting-pot. Alexandria was a place that beckoned to young and lively people of all races and creeds to come and join in its seething and infinitely varied activities.

Much of the city was magnificently constructed of stone: a Roman general later remarked that it could never be burnt down, because there was no wood to burn. Many of its buildings were world-famous—not only the Pharos, but the Museum and Library, and the temple of Sarapis. And there were also the palaces of the Ptolemies, a cluster of Greek halls and living rooms arranged round elegant parks. Remains of these buildings have now been discovered in the eastern section of the harbour area. This was where the ruling house lived, because Ptolemy I Soter, son of a Macedonian named Lagus, moved the capital to Alexandria from Memphis. Alexander had sent Ptolemy I to Egypt as his governor, and after Alexander's death he asserted his control over the country (and Cyrenaica [the region west of Egypt]) as an independent ruler, taking the Greek title of king in 305–304. His Lagid dynasty outlasted those of the other two major successor kingdoms, continuing, despite many ups and downs, until the death of Cleopatra VII in 30 B.C.

Ptolemy I's brilliant administrative powers rapidly brought the country, which had not been devastated in the recent wars, into fairly full working order. [The Greek poet] Theocritus, who hoped for Ptolemaic patronage, declared that 'Lagus' son boldly achieved such grand schemes as no man but he could ever have thought of.' And then Theocritus spoke up once again, to offer more detailed flattery of Ptolemy II Philadelphus (283–246)—who made Egypt even richer.

In their dependencies in Syria and Asia Minor the Ptolemies founded colonies in the Greek style, but they decided not to do so in Egypt, where the population was already so dense (probably between six and seven millions), and thoroughly and intricately organized on traditional lines of its own.

The exceptions were Alexandria in the north and Ptolemais Hermiou in the south. Ptolemais Hermiou was intended as a centre of Hellenism in upper [i.e., southern] Egypt, as a rival to Egyptian Thebes. And on a far larger scale that was the role of Alexandria in the north, in competition with Memphis. The purpose of Alexandria was to provide the whole country with a Greek rallying point. Ptolemy I Soter himself set a seal on the city's new status by seizing the embalmed body of Alexander the Great, and, after a brief period of lodgement at Memphis, moving it to Alexandria and laying it there with great pomp. This had been the late king's foundation, and now it was to be his permanent resting-place: its presence supported Ptolemy's claim to be, in a very special sense, Alexander's successor.

Yet Alexandria was a curious capital, because, despite its links with the interior by way of the Nile, it never quite belonged to the country; the city was not so much its centre as its superstructure. People spoke of travelling from Alexandria 'to Egypt': after its role as a Greek headquarters, its other primary function was to be the chief port of the eastern Mediterranean, the capital of an empire.

For although a Ptolemy was 'king' in the eyes of the Greeks, he was not king 'of Egypt', but (like the other Successors) king in general and undefined terms—and this situation was reflected and demonstrated by his overseas dominions. They were intended to put Egypt right back into the centre of international affairs: and the monarchs made continual endeavours to keep and increase these territories. At their most, they included Cyrenaica (with the ancient city of Cyrene), Cyprus (where the old local kingships were replaced by city-states) and many other islands; and the empire extended all along the coast of Asia Minor. But the greatest efforts had to be expended on southern Syria and Lebanon. . . .

The Ptolemaic empire served very important purposes. It was designed as an advanced screen to protect Egypt from its enemies. It was also intended to bring immense commercial profit. The Ptolemies needed a positive cash balance, based on economic self-sufficiency, in order to finance their military expenditure. And by means of their foreign dominions they were able to control a massive proportion of the Aegean market, which still played a pre-eminent part in Mediterranean and near-eastern trade. In particular, these Aegean dependencies provided pitch and metals and ships' timbers, which Egypt itself did not possess. In addition, the same lands supplied the Ptolemies with the shipwrights and navigators they so greatly needed.

But the monarchs simultaneously looked towards the south and east as well, abandoning none of the old trading routes and creating many new ones. The first four Ptolemies' seamen opened up the Red Sea and went much further afield as well, and later mariners continued to explore sea-routes of Africa and India, guarding the maritime terminals of the south Arabian caravans and suppressing the pirates who threatened the passage of their merchandise. Goods came into Egypt from the south and were re-exported into the Mediterranean area, including many materials which came in raw and unworked and left the country in manufactured form. Exports were the essence of Ptolemaic policy and profit.

The State Bureaucracy

In order to develop all such activities as efficiently as possible, it was necessary to raise internal organization to the highest pitch of vigorous productivity. Ptolemy I Soter began this task, but it was greatly developed and elaborated by his son Ptolemy II Philadelphus, who took excellent advantage of the country's temporary exemption from the blood-letting that was going on elsewhere. One of the remarkable features of his system was the creation of the most elaborate and far-reaching bureaucracy the world had ever known. And, at first, these Greek bureaucrats in Egypt served their state with efficient skill. A dominant figure in this process was the formidably active and versatile Apollonius, finance minister of the government from *c.* 268/7 for over twenty years, of whom we know a great deal from the archives of his trusted agent and estate administrator, Zeno of Caunus. This information comes to us from papyri; and indeed we owe most of our knowledge of what was happening in Egypt to such papyri, which its sands have so abundantly and uniquely preserved.

One of the most enlightening among these documents contains an official assertion that 'no one has the right to do what he wants to do, but everything is regulated for the best'! The governing idea was that the country belonged to the kings, who had the full right to use it for the general good. In pursuance of this doctrine, the Ptolemies tended to merge the civil and military power, so as to be able to organize the government and its pervasive police with ever greater thoroughness on the lines of military discipline.

Everything the monarchs did served the exploitation of all possible resources for their own advantage, subordinating the economy to state power; the whole structure was meant to buzz like a disciplined hive so that every conceivable form of enrichment could be extracted for the benefit of the king, at minimum expense. . . . In this tasks the kings were assisted by the obligatory, universal compilation of demographic and economic registers of startlingly detailed character. Through these, the government ought to have been in a position to know what most of their subjects were doing, and were worth, at any given time, although the functionaries later became swamped in their own statistics.

The system was to be seen in its most elaborate form in its application to agriculture. Spurred on by Egypt's fabulous natural resources, the first two Ptolemies were the most impressive land-improvers in Greek history. Ptolemy II Philadelphus reclaimed large tracts of desert in the Fayum, and Greek engineers introduced more scientific methods of irrigation (one of the few major technological advances of the period): so that the peasants, previously content with primitive ways of working their beneficently Nile-flooded soil, found themselves dragged sharply out of the Bronze Age into the present—that is to say, into the Iron Age, since iron tools had not been used in the country before.

A very considerable proportion of this soil was 'royal

land', belonging to the kings themselves and operated by their representatives. Exactly how large this category of land may have been, we cannot say: perhaps more, proportionately, than in any other Hellenistic monarchy, since the Ptolemies were said to be able to feed half a million people from their own estates. . . . Choice pieces of real estate were assigned to Greeks and Macedonians under the name of 'cleruchies', of which the monarch himself still retained the ultimate ownership. And in particular allotments were rented out on favourable terms—indeed, often without the need for any payment at all—to senior officers and civil servants, as incentives to loyalty, for although it was the policy of the Ptolemies to take much and give little away, they showed calculated generosity in their distribution of favours to privileged persons. . . . Moreover, royal lands were also let out (on terms varying between leniency and stiffness) to a wide range of less important individuals, often of Egyptian race, as well as to institutions, including temples, or occasionally whole urban communities. . . .

The Ptolemaic system has been described as a system of monopolistic nationalization or state socialism, perhaps the most thoroughgoing until the present century. But this is not entirely accurate. For the men directly working for the kings on their royal land form only part of the picture. The numerous remaining farmers and peasants in the country were cultivating portions of land that they had leased from the monarchs, so that the latter, although they told them in such detail what to do, were not their direct employers. It was not, that is to say, so much a monopolistic state socialism as a command economy.

The results, for a century, were unprecedented and spectacular. Their most impressive manifestation was to be seen in the production of grain, especially wheat—

which was Egypt's staple crop—but also barley. The grain, like other produce, had to be cultivated in every region according to an official timetable, annually adjusted to meet the king's requirements. This grain trade exceeded all others in importance, for it was Egypt's principal resource: in a society in which wheat and barley played a far larger part as foodstuffs than they do today, the Ptolemies were the greatest of all the grain merchants in the world, the greatest it had ever seen. Millions of bushels were exported by the kings' agents every year, using [the Greek islands of] Rhodes and Delos as their international distribution centres. . . .

Tax Collectors and Bankers

Ptolemaic taxation was equally far-reaching. A direct, uniform land tax, on the lines adopted by some other Hellenistic states, was not levied. However, the subjects of the Ptolemies paid taxes of a size and diversity that were unprecedented in the ancient world. Every detail of more than two hundred of these impositions is recorded, and Ptolemy II Philadelphus, in particular, extorted an abundance of taxation which could scarcely be equalled even today. Everyone, at every level, paid heavy taxes in order to buy from the producers, who suffered equally heavy burdens themselves. Furthermore, in order to prevent competition from other countries, not only did the Ptolemies maintain a separate coin standard all their own (the light 'Phoenician' standard), but another expedient was resorted to as well: an import tax of 50 per cent was applied to all imported oil (notably the olive-oil of Greece, superior to the local seed products). Moreover, if oil was imported all the same, it had to be sold to the king at a fixed price, cases of evasion being punished with confiscation and heavy fines. The collection of a great deal of this revenue was entrusted, for a price, to tax-farmers, middle-mcn bctwccn thc taxpayers and the government. This, as the experience of the Roman empire later showed, was a system easily liable to abuse, but the Ptolemies— at least to begin with—controlled the tax-farmers with exemplary strictness.

Taxation was one of the facts of life that prompted the Ptolemies to encourage a massive development of banking. This was already an ancient institution in the Greek world: but amid the far-flung transactions and exchange requirements of the Ptolemaic kingdom, as elsewhere in the Hellenistic world, a new and more professional kind of bank arose, replacing the old oral management of business by insistence upon written documents. Another novelty of the banking system was centralization, based on the establishment of a central state bank at Alexandria, with branches elsewhere. It was these royal institutions that guaranteed the contracts between the state and the tax-farmers; and the banks acted as receiving agents for taxes paid either in kind or in cash. They had many other functions as well. For example, it was their duty to effect payments that needed to be made from the king's treasury—and, conversely, to develop every means of bringing more wealth into its coffers. The banks also found time to look after private funds.

The Wilting of Egyptian Culture
Banks were sometimes attached to the temples, which had been, for millennia, the basic stable institutions of Egyptian society, and still remained powerful economic, intellectual and artistic units. It was only in these temple societies that the indigenous Egyptian upper class still survived; they remained the principal centres of the national civilization and script and craftsmanship, enabling the literary . . . architectural and sculptural traditions of Egypt to resist obliteration, and remain largely independent of the imported Greek culture. These survivals

were encouraged by the Ptolemies, who reduced the temples to indirect dependence upon themselves by granting them privileges and allocating them funds. In response, Manetho, the Egyptian high-priest at Heliopolis (On), wrote a history of Egypt in Greek (later added to and amended by anonymous hands) and dedicated it to Ptolemy II Philadelphus. The latter's son Ptolemy III Euergetes (246–221) made particularly strong attempts to gain favour with the native priesthood. The cults of Isis and Sarapis, which the Ptolemies indefatigably stimulated, were Hellenized versions of Egyptian traditions. In other respects, however, the monarchs accepted the separate existence of Egypt's religion just as it was, without attempting to convert or modify its ancient, native characteristics. The new rulers also wanted themselves to be seen not only as Greek kings but as Pharaohs of Egypt, and Ptolemy V Epiphanes (205–180) was crowned at Memphis according to Egyptian rites.

And yet, despite all these moves, Egyptian culture tended to wilt. For the relationship between Greeks (and Macedonians) on the one hand, and Egyptians on the other, remained fundamentally unsatisfactory. The trouble was that the Greeks enjoyed a markedly superior status. True, some of the ordinary Egyptians under the early Ptolemies were better off than they had been for a good many centuries past, since the monarchs felt it necessary to protect them from the worst oppressions—if only out of self-interest. Nor could it be said that these rulers consciously or deliberately followed racialistic principles: their policy was not racial but royal—the pursuit of their own advantage. Nevertheless, it was the Greeks who were, to an overwhelming extent, the principal agents and supports of their régime, and this situation inevitably made itself felt and caused friction.

The Greeks, it is true, were impressed by the antiquity of Egypt. . . . Moreover, the poorer members of their community sometimes intermarried with Egyptians, at least from the time of Ptolemy II Philadelphus onwards. Yet the Greeks had brought with them into the country the conviction that every individual Egyptian was violent and dishonest, and it was a conviction that most of them persistently retained. Greek judges were grossly biased against Egyptians. Native peasants—who cheaply performed the lowest kinds of manual labour, reserved for slaves in other countries—paid much heavier taxes than Greek residents, and lived virtually in a state of profitless bondage. . . .

The Ptolemies in Decline

Besides, the successes of the Ptolemaic economy did not last. For the centralized, bureaucratic system could only work adequately under men who possessed exceptional drive—and were immune from ordinary human failings. For a time the former requirement was met. But in the nature of things this could not go on for ever, and the Egyptians, under the impact of increasing ill-treatment, inevitably became dangerously embittered, and finally desperate. The deterioration was gradual, and uneven. But already in the reign of Ptolemy II Philadelphus, the correspondence of Apollonius' agent Zeno of Caunus shows that discrimination could be found, and was resented. 'I do not know how to behave like a Greek (*hellenizein*)' mourns a camel-driver (perhaps an Arab). And under Ptolemy III Euergetes, a priest complains that the Greek billeted in his home looks down on him 'because he is an Egyptian'. . . . Native revolts broke out, and then proved impossible to stop. For two decades (208/7-187/6), almost the whole of the Thebaid in Upper Egypt, always the breeding-ground for Pharaonic nationalism, fell under the independent rule of secessionist Nubian kings, and the breakaway was only terminated by Ptolemy V Epiphanes (205–180) amid savage repression. This was an epoch of chaotic local uprisings, sieges and robberies; and Nile transport became perilously insecure. In these years, moreover, it was not only the Egyptians but the ruling race who felt unsafe; for example, a recluse (named Ptolemy) is found complaining that he has been assaulted because he is a Macedonian. Furthermore, Ptolemy V's loss of most of his imperial possessions to the Seleucid Antiochus IV Epiphanes at the battle of Panion (200) isolated Egypt from its eastern commerce, and thus caused even worse impoverishment. Besides, the dynastic quarrels and court scandals that characterized the next reigns—in addition to new bouts of currency inflation (174–3)—meant that the welfare of the Egyptian populace declined still further.

The workers on the land had already formed the habit of registering their protests by the withdrawal of their labour—not for better wages or conditions, because clearly these were not to be had, but merely out of total despair: which was converted into this sort of protest action, from time to time, by some fortuitous irritation or hold-up. But as the second century B.C. continued on its way, something much more serious began to happen as well. For the peasants (and even tax-farmers unable to meet their obligations) increasingly went on strike by fleeing from their jobs and homes, usually in groups, and taking refuge in sanctuaries or going underground. 'We are worn out,' declares a papyrus letter, 'we will run away.' And so the economic recession got worse still, because now there were not enough people left to cultivate the soil. Ptolemy VIII Euergetes II, who had the reputation of favouring the native population, produced a remarkable decree (not the first of its kind) ordering . . . amnesties, the lightening of burdens, tax exemptions, counsels of moderation to officials. But it was too late. Egypt continued to lurch towards collapse and dependence on unscrupulous Romans—and on Rome itself. . . .

One of the worst problems that confronted the authorities—and these profit-seeking Roman adventurers as well—was the condition of the vast city of Alexandria. Its Graeco-Macedonian population had by now become a mixed race of exceptional liveliness, addicted to over-excitement and rioting. The palace, too, was sometimes in the hands of shady personages, notably the cunning and murderous Sosibius and his friends, who directed the régime of Ptolemy IV Philopator; and subsequently the court, although it remained Greek in culture, was dominated—like the courts of eastern states—by eunuchs, who were sometimes of sinister character. This volatile Alexandria was the powerbase of Cleopatra VII Philadelphus Philopator Philopatris, who came to the throne in 51 B.C. and made a last determined attempt to revive the kingdom and empire by means of her successive associations with Julius Caesar (allegedly the father of her son, Ptolemy XV Caesar or Caesarion) and then Marcus Antonius (Antony) (by whom she had additional children). But the attempt failed—shortly before the last Indo-Greek kingdom, too, had collapsed—and after nearly three hundred years of Ptolemaic kingship the country became a Roman province in 30 B.C. In spite of all the disasters it had suffered, it was still rich enough, especially in grain, to revolutionize the Roman economy. During the rule of the Romans, however, the Egyptian people did not fare even as well as they had under the Ptolemaic house—or at least under its earlier monarchs.

Cleopatra: A Legendary Queen

Peter Green

By the mid–first century B.C., Ptolemaic Egypt had shrunk into a third-rate power cowering in Rome's great shadow. This was the age of devastating civil wars and power struggles among powerful individuals, including the renowned Roman generals Julius Caesar and Gnaeus Pompey; Caesar's lieutenant, Marcus Antonius (Mark Antony); and Caesar's adopted son, Octavian (the future emperor Augustus). To their number must be added one Greek, who was every bit as talented and ambitious as they—Cleopatra VII, daughter of Ptolemy XII. After she and her lover/ally Antony went down to defeat at Actium in western Greece in 31 B.C., she became the last of the Ptolemies, the last independent Greek ruler of antiquity, and the last of Egypt's independent pharaohs. As Peter Green of the University of Texas at Austin points out in this excerpt from his definitive study of the Hellenistic Greeks, it was perhaps poetically fitting that the era's first and last great Greek figures—Alexander the Great and Cleopatra—both became and remain legendary.

🐝 🐝 🐝

Peter Green, *Alexander to Actium: The Historical Evolution of the Hellenistic Age.* Berkeley: University of California Press, 1990. Copyright © 1990 by Peter Green. Reproduced by permission of the publisher.

One of the more tempting excuses for Rome's progressively more radical, steadily less reluctant policy of intervention and eventual takeover in the eastern Mediterranean was, beyond any doubt, the patent inability of the rulers *in situ* [then in place] to manage their own affairs. This not only encouraged what Rome, and conservatives generally, saw as dangerous sociopolitical trends—mass movements by the dispossessed, encroachment by non-Mediterranean tribal elements—but, worse, proved disastrous for trade, a fault that Roman administrative paternalism could seldom resist the temptation to correct. In addition to the rampant scourge of piracy . . . a general condition of acute economic and, intermittently, political anarchy now afflicted both Syria and Egypt. Cities, local chieftains, and individuals all broke away when they could from a now highly inefficient (though no less captious and oppressive) system of central bureaucracy. Endless . . . dynastic conflicts, combined with relentless extortion (to pay for these and other excesses), had all but destroyed the countryside.

Since both Syria and Egypt were potentially the most fertile and productive areas imaginable, this represented a more than usually monumental feat of short-sighted stupidity—and indeed one is constantly amazed at just how much, even *in extremis*, could still be extracted from the inhabitants to meet yet another crisis. Alexandria, of course, had the advantage, in addition, of still-substantial royal treasures. In 59 Ptolemy XII Auletes raised almost six thousand talents, perhaps a year's revenue, perhaps less, to bribe Caesar, now consul, into successfully upholding his claim to recognition by the Senate. . . . Though some of this money was raised through a loan, or loans, from the Roman banker Gaius Rabirius Postumus, the rest came from Ptolemy's own resources, while the loans were recouped by extorting extra funds from his long-suffering subjects. His annual revenues, indeed, were variously estimated at between six and twelve and a half thousand talents. . . . This was a situation that positively invited Rome's attention. Unfortunately . . . the profit principle proved no less irresistible to Roman administrators, businessmen, and, all too soon, senators than it had done to the Macedonians. The tradition, after all, was well established. It had been what panhellenism was all about, as early as the fourth century: a united ethnic crusade against the East, with wealth and power as its objectives, cultural superiority (and Xerxes' long-past invasion) as its justification. That had been the whole moral basis of Alexander's expedition, of the sharing of the spoils by his successors. Material greed and racial contempt had been the fuel that maintained Macedonians in power, from the Nile to the Euphrates, for three centuries—while their own *mores* steadily degenerated, and, more subtly, were infiltrated by the culture of those whose capital they stole, whose languages they ignored. Now, with the Romans—whom Alexander's descendants, prematurely, also dismissed as mere barbarians—the situation was abruptly reversed: it was Rome that very soon began to display contempt for these effete and fractious dynasts. . . .

Ptolemy the Piper

Behind the last convulsive struggles of Seleucids and Ptolemies Roman policy—or, worse, free enterprise minus a policy—can always be sensed in the background. Worse still, from the viewpoint of the Greeks in particular, was the imposition of rival foreign warlords—Caesar and Pompey, Octavian and Antony—who not only fought out their own dynastic struggles on Greek soil and in Greek waters, but bled the inhabitants white for supplies, from grain to warships, and had an unnerving habit of executing those who chose the wrong (i.e., the unsuccessful) side. Roman egotism was matched, as so often, by Greek cynicism: survival became the prime objective. . . .

If Ptolemy Auletes . . . enjoyed a relatively undisturbed reign of almost thirty years (80–59/8, 55–51) in which to indulge his passion for flute playing (*Aulētēs* means "Piper") and other, less mentionable, habits, that was no tribute to his strength of character. . . . There were, in fact, two good reasons why Ptolemy Auletes, and his kingdom, survived as long as they did. To begin with, he had no serious rivals for the throne. This did not mean he was popular—far from it—but it did set his enemies a problem when it came to replacing him. At the time of his enforced exile in 59/8 . . . the Alexandrians—who had thrown him out . . . scraped the very bottom of the dynastic barrel trying to find any acceptable substitute for him.

After a little-known son of Cleopatra Selene [a former royal princess, daughter of Ptolemy X] had died on them during negotiations, . . . in desperation they picked on an alleged royal claimant whose chief title to consideration was the name of Seleucus. His appearance, and oafish manners, got him the nickname in Alexandria of *Kybiosaktēs*, "the Salt-Fish Hawker." The ulterior purpose of this frantic search was to find a male consort for Auletes' daughter Berenice, who had been proclaimed queen in her father's absence, perhaps at first as a temporary measure. The evidence is patchy. . . . Auletes left behind, as co-regents in his absence, his wife (and sister) Cleopatra V Tryphaena, together with their eldest daughter, Berenice IV. Two other daughters, Arsinoë and Cleopatra VII, the future queen, were barely adolescent, while the boys, Ptolemy XIII and Ptolemy XIV, were still infants. . . .

Enter Cleopatra

[These last members of the Ptolemaic dynasty] went out in a blaze of glory that has inspired great poetry down the ages. In the spring of 51 Ptolemy Auletes died, leaving the kingdom in his will, jointly, to his eighteen-year-old daughter Cleopatra, and her younger brother Ptolemy XIII, then about twelve. In Cleopatra the tradition of brilliant, strong-willed Macedonian queens reached its apotheosis. With Cyprus, Coele-Syria, and Cyrenaica gone, with the world her ancestors had known crumbling about her, with famine at home and anarchy abroad, this astonishing woman not only dreamed of greater world empire than Alexander had known, but came within an iota of winning it. . . . No one could fail to take her seriously. How far her sexual allure was exercised for its own sake, and how far in pursuit of power, we shall never know for certain. But there are one or two pointers. Like many Hellenistic queens, she was passionate, but never promiscuous. Caesar and Antony apart, we hear of no other lovers. . . . The wretched surviving iconography [surviving images of her on coins and so on] suggests neither a raving beauty nor a voluptuary. . . . There is also her choice of lovers to consider. Anyone who so consistently aimed for the top is unlikely to have been motivated by nothing apart from sheer unbridled passion. . . . She was, in short, a charismatic personality of the first order, a born leader and vaultingly ambitious monarch, who deserved a better fate than suicide. . . .

The times, however, were hard, and she was forced to make of them what she could—which was a great deal. The civil wars in Italy [between Caesar and Pompey] broke out in 49, two years after she came to the throne. She made her independent spirit clear from the start. By August 51 she had already dropped her young brother's name from official documents, despite traditional Ptolemaic insistence on titular male precedence among co-rulers. (Throughout her reign, independent or not, Cleopatra was always forced to accept either a brother or a son, however underage or otherwise ineffectual, as obligatory consort: there were some traditions not even she could ignore.) She also, exceptionally, put her own portrait and name on her coinage, again ignoring those of her brother. This, not surprisingly, alarmed the more powerful court officials in Alexandria. . . . Such behavior very soon brought opposition to a head. Certainly by 48, and in all likelihood two years earlier, a palace cabal [plot], led by Theodotus, the eunuch Pothinus, and a half-Greek general, Achillas, ousted Cleopatra in favor of her more pliable younger brother, with themselves as a council of regency. . . .

Enter Caesar

Meanwhile Pompey, defeated at Pharsalus (Aug. 48), took ship for Alexandria. He was relying, unwisely, on his position as backer, indeed as Senate-appointed guardian, of young Ptolemy XIII. . . . He seems not to have realized, till it was too late, just how far Pharsalus had destroyed his international reputation and credit. Achillas and his fellow regents were already working out their best approach to Caesar; in their eyes Pompey was nothing but a dangerous embarrassment. They had him murdered as he stepped ashore (28 Sept. 48), an object lesson for the precocious boy king, who watched this scene from the dockside, arrayed in his diadem and purple robes. Pompey's severed head was pickled, and afterwards presented, as an earnest of good will, to his conqueror, who at least had the grace to shed tears at the sight. Caesar may have been only too glad to have Pompey thus providentially put out of the way, but the circumstances of his death were appalling, and Caesar himself knew this better than anyone. At the same time the episode encouraged him in what was to prove a near-fatal Egyptian adventure. When he came ashore himself at Alexandria four days later (2 Oct.), he was in a mood of careless and arrogant confidence, with an escort of no more than thirty-two hundred legionaries and eight hundred cavalry. His public reception was anything but ecstatic. . . . Riots followed.

Ptolemy XIII was away at Pelusium, ready to defend

A young woman kneels before Cleopatra to offer flowers. Cleopatra was a strong-willed queen who dreamed of a greater world empire.

the frontier against his elder sister. Caesar coolly installed himself in the royal palace and began issuing orders. Pothinus the eunuch . . . brought Ptolemy back to court, but took no steps to disband his army. At this point Cleopatra, anxious not to be left out of any deal being cut, had herself smuggled through these hostile lines, like contraband, and turned up in her carpet. Both she and her brother were invited to appear before Caesar's *ad hoc* judgment seat the following morning; but by then Caesar, who was instantly captivated by Cleopatra's insistent charms, had already made her his lover, as she doubtless intended he should. Young Ptolemy instantly grasped the situation (hardly difficult, in the circumstances), and rushed out in a fury, screaming that he had been betrayed, to rouse the Alexandrian mob. . . .

The so-called Alexandrian War, which followed . . . came as near to destroying Caesar himself, let alone his reputation, as any campaign, military or political, that he ever fought. Once he had to swim from the mole to save his life, leaving his purple general's cloak behind as a trophy for the enemy. The warehouses and some part of the great Alexandrian Library went up in flames. Caesar managed to capture the Pharos lighthouse, which safeguarded his control of the harbor. Arsinoë, meanwhile, contrived to escape from the palace, fled to Achillas, and was promptly proclaimed queen by the army and the Macedonian mob, an act for which her sister never forgave her. All through that winter fighting and intrigue sputtered on. . . . [Eventually, Caesar's forces prevailed and] Ptolemy XIII fled and was drowned in the Nile. Thus Cleopatra, whom Caesar had restored, officially, to joint occupancy of the throne of Egypt, now, in effect, indeed became sole ruler—although as a sop to tradition she was duly married off to her younger brother Ptolemy XIV, now aged eleven. . . .

Rather than make Egypt a province, with all the senatorial intrigue and rivalry that this was bound to entail, Caesar had every intention of shoring up the Ptolemaic regime, on his own terms. To have a son in line for the throne would by no means come amiss, whatever the status of consort and heir in Rome. Meanwhile, to placate the Alexandrians and the Egyptian priesthood, Cleopatra obligingly wed her sibling co-regent, while her younger sister, Arsinoë languished under arrest with a charge of high treason pending against her. . . .

In July 46, after his successful African campaign, Caesar returned to Rome, to be showered with unprecedented honors, including four successive triumphs and a ten-year dictatorship. During these celebrations (Sept.–Oct.) he brought over Cleopatra and her entourage, establishing them in his own town house, a return of hospitality that caused considerable offense among conservative Republicans. . . . By then he was mulling over ideas about deification and world empire that seemed, or were thought, to include the establishment of Alexandria as a second capital, and of Cleopatra herself as some kind of bigamous queen-goddess, the New Isis, as she styled herself. Rome buzzed with gossip. . . .

Exit Caesar, Enter Antony

But the Ides of March 44 [when Caesar was stabbed to death in the Senate] put an end to all these grandiose dreams. Two weeks after Caesar's assassination, when the will was known and Caesarion [her young son by Caesar] inevitably, had no place in it, Cleopatra, with more speed than dignity, and perhaps in real danger of her life, left Rome and returned to Alexandria. . . . On her arrival Cleopatra lost no time in having her sibling consort, Ptolemy XIV, assassinated, and Caesarion established, at the tender age of four, as her new coregent. [Soon afterward, Octavian and Antony defeated Caesar's assassins and Cleopatra, like many others at the time, saw Antony as the most likely person to control the Roman sphere.] . . .

By the time that Antony summoned her to that fateful meeting at Tarsus, in 41, she already knew more than enough about him: his limited tactical and strategic abilities, his great popularity with his troops; his blue blood, which was so embarrassingly offset by financial impoverishment; the drinking, the . . . womanizing, the . . . Herculean vulgarity, the physical exuberance and brutal ambition, the Dionysiac pretensions to godhead. . . .

Antony was tickled by the idea of having a blue-blooded Ptolemy (his previous mistresses, not to mention his present wife, Fulvia, a powerful termagant, all seem to have been shrewishly middle-class), and by the coarse implications of all this royal finery: eight or nine years later we find him writing to Octavian, asking him why he has changed so much, turned so hostile—"Is it because I get into the queen?". . .

Both Cleopatra and Antony, then, had highly practical ulterior reasons for cultivating one another; how much personal chemistry helped the equation is hard to tell. Nor can anyone be certain how soon Antony planned to return when he left Cleopatra in the early spring of 40, or what he told her—not necessarily the same thing. Her magnetism was by no means irresistible, since in the event he did not see her for another four years. . . . Public considerations once more came first. That same autumn Antony made his peace with Octavian at Brundisium (Brindisi), cemented the alliance by marrying his fellow triumvir's sister, Octavia—a beautiful and high-minded young intellectual, recently widowed, and with three children from her first marriage. . . . Meanwhile in Alexandria Cleopatra, never one to do things by halves, bore Antony twins, a boy and a girl. His first child by Octavia, a girl, was born in 38.

Just what Antony thought he was doing at this point is not wholly clear. He may have been playing the Roman card; he may have thought he could finesse Cleopatra against Octavia, in whose company, during the winter of 38–37, he played the dutiful intellectual in Athens, attending lectures and going the rounds of the philosophical schools. . . . Octavian's growing enmity also must have turned him back toward the idea of playing winner-take-all, with Alexandria as his base. If Octavia had borne him a son, things might have been different; but she had not, and Cleopatra had. Cleopatra also held the still-impressive accumulated treasure of the Ptolemies, something that Octavian, too, kept very much in mind. . . .

So Antony left Italy and went east, with the Senate's authority to reallocate client kingdoms—a commission that, as we shall see, he proceeded to interpret in a more than liberal fashion. . . . The first thing that Antony did, on reaching Antioch, was to send for Cleopatra. After their long separation it was now that his, or their, schemes for . . . a "Romano-Hellenistic Orient" began to take shape.

Antony proceeded to lavish on the queen not only Cyprus . . . but also the cedar-clad Cilician coast, so ideal for shipbuilding, not to mention Phoenicia, Coele-Syria, and the richest spice-bearing regions of Judaea and Arabia, dispositions that not unnaturally caused vast offense in Rome, and not only because of Cleopatra's personal unpopularity there: these provincial areas were in fact not in his authority to dispose of, and the obvious purpose of their allocation to Cleopatra, Egypt itself being virtually without timber, was to provide lumber and shipyards for the creation of a large Egyptian fleet. The twin children were also now acknowledged by Antony, and officially named Alexander Helios and Cleopatra Selene, titles powerfully evocative of Hellenistic dynastic ambition. . . .

So it came about that in 34 Antony committed himself still further to his independent Graeco-Roman dream. After a successful—and financially rewarding—Armenian campaign he celebrated a triumphal parade through Alexandria, playing the role of the New Dionysus, while Cleopatra, enthroned as the New Isis, presided over the ceremony. (Inevitably, when the news reached Rome, this occasion was misinterpreted as an unauthorized and improper Roman triumph.) Only a few days later a yet more explicit political ceremony took place. In the great Gymnasium of Alexandria, with Cleopatra once more robed as Isis, and Antony enthroned by her side, titles were bestowed upon the royal children. Ptolemy XV Caesar (Caesarion)—though carefully subordinated to the royal pair—was made joint ruler of Egypt with his mother and proclaimed King of Kings (she became Queen of Kings, a higher honor still). Alexander Helios . . . was declared Great King of what had been the Seleucid empire at its zenith. . . . His sister, Cleopatra Selene, was instated as Queen of Cyrenaica and Crete. The youngest son of Antony and Cleopatra, Ptolemy Philadelphos . . . was proclaimed, at the age of two, King of Syria and Asia Minor: he was also dressed in Macedonian royal robes. . . .

[These ceremonies] not only laid improper claim to territories that were either outside Rome's control or, worse, already under Roman administration; they also made it only too clear that Cleopatra and the formidable resources of Egypt were backing Antony's dreams. Once again the irresistible lure of world empire was in the air: the grim lessons of the past three centuries had been quickly forgotten. . . .

Enter Octavian, Exit Antony, Cleopatra, and an Independent Egypt

In 32/1 Antony formally divorced Octavia, thus forcing the West to recognize his relationship with Cleopatra; he had already, unprecedentedly, put the Egyptian queen's head and name on his official Roman coinage, the silver denarii that enjoyed an enormously wide circulation throughout the eastern Mediterranean. These acts also terminated even the pretense of his Roman allegiance, and Octavian . . . formally declared war on Cleopatra, and on her alone; no mention was made of Antony. The whipped-up hysterical xenophobia [antiforeign feelings] current in Rome at the time can be sensed from the (largely factitious) propaganda of such Augustan poets as Virgil and Propertius. Cleopatra was the drunken lascivious Oriental, worked over by her own house slaves, . . . whoring after strange gods and foreign ways. . . . Inevitably, she was also portrayed as an indiscriminately sensual harlot, a charge that, as we have seen, was almost certainly false, though she did (it was claimed) derive a "really sensuous pleasure" from literature.

Antony became the target of more serious, and better founded, political accusations, for example that he had misused troops, acted without senatorial authorization, and given away territories that belonged to Rome. . . .

The exaggerated charges against Cleopatra also reveal fear; and though today the outcome may seem inevitable . . . at the time many must have believed that the New Isis would triumph, that Antony would indeed launch a dazzling new career of world conquest and imperial co-partnership from Alexandria. . . . Octavian's crushing naval victory at Actium, on 2 September 31— planned and won for him by his admiral Agrippa—finally put paid to Antony's ambitions. Less than a year later, after a halfhearted defense of Alexandria against Octavian's advancing army, Antony committed suicide.

Cleopatra soon followed his example. . . . Once she was safely dead, admiring tributes to her noble end could be entertained without risk, while her heir Caesarion was butchered without compunction.

On 29 August, 30 B.C., Octavian officially declared the Ptolemaic dynasty at an end, thus writing finis—as we can see now—to the whole Hellenistic era of the Successors. . . . The Successors' territories, meanwhile, were absorbed into the administrative efficiency of a semi-Stoicized universal empire. No room, there, for the New Isis. Yet Cleopatra achieved her dying wish. Unlike her forebears, she knew the country she ruled; and when she had the famous asp—in fact an Egyptian cobra—smuggled to her in a basket of figs, it was in the belief that, as Egyptian religion declared, death from snakebite would, the . . . cobra being sacred, confer immortality. She was not mistaken. Only Alexander—another Macedonian—could eclipse the mesmeric fascination that she exercised down the centuries, and still exercises, upon the European imagination: the perennial symbol of what, had Actium gone the other way, might have been a profoundly different world. We end, as we began, with a legend.

Cleopatra's Dreams Shattered: The Battle of Actium

Dio Cassius

Following is the most complete surviving ancient description of the naval encounter at Actium in 31 B.C., the battle that effectively ended Cleopatra's and Antony's dreams of a new world order and decided the fate of the Roman world for many years to come. It was written by the Romanized Greek historian Dio Cassius (ca. A.D. 150–235), who had a distinguished political career as a Roman official, serving as a senator, twice as consul in Rome (in 205 and 229), and also as governor of the provinces of Dalmatia and Africa. The work for which he is best known is a large-scale history of Rome in eighty books (written in Greek), from which this tract is excerpted.

❧ ❧ ❧

[O]ctavian] drew up a plan to allow Antony's ships to sail through, and then to attack from the rear as they fled. For his part, he hoped that his vessels could muster enough speed to capture Antony and Cleopatra quickly, and he calculated that once it became clear that they were trying to escape, he could, through their action, persuade the rest to surrender without fighting. But this scheme was opposed by Agrippa, who feared that their ships, which were using oars, would be too slow to catch the fugitives, who intended to hoist sails. Also a violent rainstorm accompanied by a tremendous wind had in the meanwhile struck Antony's fleet, leaving it in total confusion, though it had not touched his own, and this gave him some confidence that he would win easily enough. So he abandoned his plan, and, like Antony, posted large numbers of infantry on his ships. He also embarked his subordinates in auxiliary craft: they were to move rapidly between the ships, giving the necessary instructions to the men in action, and reporting back all that he needed to know. Then he waited for the enemy to sail out.

At the sound of the trumpet Antony's fleet began to move, and, keeping close together, formed their line a little way outside the strait, but then advanced no further. Octavian put out, as if to engage should the enemy stand their ground, or else to make them retire. But when they neither came out against him, nor turned away, but stayed in position and even increased the density of their closely packed formation, Octavian halted his advance, being in doubt as to what to do. He ordered his rowers to let their oars rest in the water, and waited for a while; after this he suddenly made a signal and, advancing both his wings, rounded his line in the form of an enveloping crescent. His object was to encircle the enemy if possible, or, if not, at least to break up their formation. Antony was alarmed by this outflanking and encircling manoeuvre, moved forward to meet it as best he could, and so unwillingly joined battle with Octavian.

So the fleets came to grips and the battle began. Each side uttered loud shouts to the men aboard, urging the troops to summon up their prowess and their fighting spirit, and the men could also hear a babel of orders being shouted at them from those on shore.

The two sides used different tactics. Octavian's fleet, having smaller and faster ships, could advance at speed and ram the enemy, since their armour gave them protection on all sides. If they sank a vessel, they had achieved their object; if not, they would back water before they could be engaged at close quarters, and either ram the same ship suddenly a second time, or let it go and turn against others. When they had damaged these as much as they could in a short time, they would seek out fresh opponents over and over again, constantly switching their attack, so that their onslaught always came where it was least expected. They feared their adversaries' long-range missiles no less than their superior strength in fighting at close quarters, and so they wasted no time either in the approach or the clash. They would sail up suddenly so as to close with their target before the enemy's archers could hit them, inflict damage or cause enough confusion to escape being grappled, and then quickly back away out of range.

Antony's tactics, on the other hand, were to pour heavy volleys of stones and arrows upon the enemy ships as they approached, and then try to entrap them with iron grapnels. When they could reach their targets, Antony's ships got the upper hand, but if they missed, their own hulls would be pierced by the rams and they would sink, or else, in the attempt to avoid collision, they would lose time and expose themselves to attack by other ships. Two or three of Octavian's vessels would fall upon one of Antony's, with some inflicting all the damage they could, while the others bore the brunt of the counter-attack.

On the one side the helmsmen and rowers suffered the heaviest casualties, on the other the marines. Octavian's ships resembled cavalry, now launching a charge, and now retreating, since they could attack or draw off as they chose, while Antony's were like heavy infantry, warding off the enemy's efforts to ram them, but also striving to hold them with their grappling-hooks. Each fleet in turn gained the advantage over the other: the one would dart in against the rows of oars which projected from the ships' sides and break the blades, while the other fighting from its higher decks would sink its adversaries with stones and ballistic missiles. At the same time each side had its weaknesses. Antony's ships could do no damage to the enemy as they approached: Octavian's, if they failed to sink a vessel when they had rammed it, would find the odds turned against them once they were grappled.

For a long while the struggle was evenly poised and neither side could gain the upper hand anywhere, but the end came in the following way. Cleopatra, whose ship was riding at anchor behind the battle lines, could not endure the long hours of uncertainty while the issue hung in the balance: both as a woman and as an Egyptian she found herself stretched to breaking-point by the agony of the suspense, and the constant and unnerving effort of picturing victory or defeat. Suddenly she made her choice—to flee—and made the signal for the others, her own subjects. So when her ships immediately hoisted their sails and stood out to sea, a favourable wind having luckily got up, Antony supposed that they were turning tail, not on Cleopatra's orders, but out of fear because they felt themselves to have been defeated, and so he followed them.

At this, dismay and confusion spread to the rest of Antony's men, and they resolved likewise to take whatever means of escape lay open. Some raised their sails, while others threw the turrets and heavy equipment overboard to lighten the vessels and help them to get away. While they were thus engaged, their opponents again attacked: they had not pursued Cleopatra's fleeing squadron, because they themselves had not taken sails aboard and had put out prepared only for a naval battle. This meant that there were many ships to attack each one of Antony's, both at long range and alongside. The result was that the struggle took many forms on both sides and was carried on with the greatest ferocity. Octavian's soldiers battered the lower parts of the ships from stem to stern, smashed the oars, broke off the rudders, and, climbing on to the decks, grappled with their enemies. They dragged down some, thrust others overboard, and fought hand to hand with others, since they now equalled them in numbers. Antony's men forced their attackers back with boat-hooks, cut them down with axes, hurled down stones and other missiles which had been prepared for this purpose, forced down those who tried to scale the ships' sides, and engaged all who came within reach. A witness of the battle might have compared it, if one can reduce the scale, to the spectacle of a number of walled towns or islands set close together being besieged from the sea. Thus one side strove to clamber up the sides of the ships, as it might be up a cliff or fortress, and brought to bear all the equipment which is needed for such an assault, while the others struggled to repel them, using all the weapons and tactics which are known to defenders.

As the fighting remained evenly balanced, Octavian, who found himself in doubt what to do next, sent for fire from his camp. Until then he had been unwilling to use it, since he was anxious to capture Antony's treasure intact. He now resorted to it because he saw that it was impossible to win in any other way and believed that this was the only weapon which would help him. The battle then changed its character. The attackers would approach their targets from many different points at once, bombarding them with blazing missiles and hurling by hand javelins with torches attached to them; from a longer range they would also catapult jars filled with charcoal or pitch. The defenders tried to ward off these missiles one by one, but when some got through, they ignited the timbers and immediately started a blaze, as is bound to happen on a ship. The crews first put out the flames with the drinking water which they carried on board, and when that ran out, they used sea water. If they managed to throw this on the fire in great quantities at once, they could sometimes quench it by the sheer volume of the water. But this was not always possible, since their buckets were few and of no great size. In their confusion they sometimes only half filled them, and in that case instead of reducing the blaze they only increased it, since small quantities of salt water poured on a fire make it burn all the more strongly. So when they found that they were failing to check the flames, they threw on their heavy cloaks and even dead bodies, and for a time these stifled the conflagration, which seemed to die down. But later, and especially when the wind blew strongly, the flames leaped up more violently than ever, fed by their own efforts.

So long as only a section of the ship was on fire, the men would stand close by and jump into it, cutting away some of the planks and scattering others; in some instances the men threw the timbers into the sea, and in others against their adversaries, in the hope that they might cause them some hurt. Others would take up position in the part of the ship that was undamaged, and would ply their long spears and grappling-hooks more desperately than ever, in the hope of making some enemy ship fast to theirs and boarding her, or, if not, setting her alight as well. But when none of the enemy came near enough, since they were guarding against this very possibility, and when the fire spread to the encircling sides of the ship and descended into the hold, they found themselves in the most terrible plight of all. Some, especially the sailors, were overcome by the smoke before the flames ever came near them, while others were roasted in the midst of the holocaust as if they were in ovens. Others were incinerated in their armour as it grew red-hot. Others, again, to avoid such a fate, or when they were half burned, threw off their armour and were wounded by the missiles shot at them from long range, or jumped into the sea and were drowned, or were clubbed by their enemies and sank, or were devoured by sea-monsters. The only men to find a death which was endurable in the midst of such sufferings were those who either killed one another in return for the service, or took their own lives before such a fate could befall them. These were spared the torments I have described, and their corpses were burned on board the ships, as though they were on a funeral pyre.

When Octavian's men saw that the battle had taken this turn, they at first held off from the enemy, since some of the latter could still defend themselves. But when the fire had taken hold of the ships, and the men aboard them, so far from being able to injure an opponent, could no longer even defend themselves, they eagerly sailed up to Antony's vessels in the hope of seizing their treasure, and tried to put out the fires which they themselves had started. The result was that many of them perished, both from the flames and from their own greed.

The Last Pharaoh's Final Days

Dio Cassius

Cleopatra's death marked the end of the long line of pharaohs who had ruled Egypt for more than three thousand years. It also turned out to be one of the most dramatic and memorable death scenes in history, one later re-created repeatedly in literature and films. This account of the event, one of several ancient ones that have survived, is by the second-century A.D. Romanized Greek historian Dio Cassius.

🐝 🐝 🐝

[A]fter Antony's death, Cleopatra] now believed that she could place some degree of trust in Octavian and at once sent word to him of what had happened, and yet she could not feel completely confident that no harm would befall her. She therefore remained in seclusion within the building, so that even if there were no other reason for keeping her alive, she could at least trade upon Octavian's fear concerning her treasure to obtain a pardon and keep her throne. Even when she had sunk to such depths of misfortune, she remembered that she was queen and preferred to die bearing the title and majesty of a sovereign rather than live in a private station. At any rate she kept ready fire to destroy her treasure, and asps and other reptiles to end her life; she had experimented before on human beings to discover how these creatures caused death in each case.

Now Octavian was much concerned not only to make himself master of her wealth, but also to capture her alive and lead her in his triumph at Rome. However, as he had given her a pledge of a kind, he did not wish to be seen as having tricked her; rather he wanted to make her appear as his captive, who had been to some extent subdued against her will. He therefore sent Gaius Proculeius, a knight, and Epaphroditus, a freedman, to visit her, and instructed them carefully as to what they should say and do. The two accordingly obtained an audience with Cleopatra, began by discussing a number of reasonable proposals, and then, before anything had been agreed, suddenly laid hands on her. After this they removed from her any means of ending her life, and allowed her to spend some days in the monument where she was engaged in embalming Antony's body. They moved her to the palace, but did not dismiss any of her accustomed retinue or attendants: their object was that she should continue to cherish the hope of obtaining her wishes, and so do nothing to harm herself. At any rate, when she sought an audience with Octavian, her request was granted, and to further the deception he promised that he would visit her himself.

So she prepared a superbly decorated apartment and a richly ornamented couch, dressed herself with studied negligence—indeed her appearance in mourning wonderfully enhanced her beauty—and seated herself on the couch. Beside her she arranged many different portraits and busts of Julius Caesar, and in her bosom she carried all the letters Caesar had sent her.

Octavian Visits Cleopatra

Then as Octavian entered, she sprang to her feet, blushed, and cried, 'Greetings, my lord, for now the gods have given supremacy to you and taken it from me. But now you can see with your own eyes how Caesar looked when he visited me so many times and you have heard tell of how he honoured me and made me queen of Egypt. You should learn something of me from his own words; these are the letters which he wrote with his own hand: take them and read them.'

So saying, she went on to read many of Caesar's passionate expression of his feelings for her. At one moment she would weep and kiss the letters and then she would kneel and bow her head before Caesar's portraits. She kept turning her eyes towards Octavian and lamenting her fate in a plaintive musical tone. Her voice melted as she murmured, 'How can thy letters, Caesar, help me now?' and 'And yet in this man thou livest for me again,' then, 'Would that I had died before thee,' and still again, 'But if I have him, I have thee.'

Such were the subtle tones of speech and changes of expression with which she addressed Octavian, casting sweet looks towards him and murmuring tender words. Octavian understood the passion with which she was speaking and the seductive power of her gestures; however, he acted as if he were unaware of these, looked towards the ground and merely replied, 'Do not distress yourself, lady, take heart, no harm shall come to you.' But her spirits were utterly cast down, because he neither looked at her, nor made any mention of her kingdom, nor uttered so much as a word of love. She threw herself on her knees, burst out weeping, and said, 'I have no desire to live, nor can I live. But this favour I beg of you, in memory of your father, that since the gods gave me to Antony after him, I too may die with Antony. I wish that I had perished at the very instant after Caesar's death. But seeing that it was my fate to suffer that parting from him, send me to Antony. Do not grudge that I should be buried with him: as I die because of him, so may I live with him, even in Hades.'

So she spoke, in the hope of arousing his pity, but Octavian made no reply. As he was afraid that she might still end her own life, he urged her yet again to take heart. After this he did not dismiss any of her attendants, but treated her with especial care in his desire that she should make a brilliant spectacle at his triumph. She guessed that this was his plan, and since she felt such a fate to be worse than any number of deaths, she now truly longed to die. She begged Octavian time and again that her life should be ended by one means or another, and of her own accord she thought of many ways to bring this about. Finally, when she could put none of these into effect, she professed to have undergone a change of heart and to place great hopes for the future both in Octavian and in Livia [Octavian's wife]. She said that she would sail to Rome of her own free will, and prepared a number of specially treasured chosen ornaments to take as gifts. In this way she hoped to convince them that she did not intend to die, and hence that she would be less closely guarded and thus enabled to kill herself.

So it came about. As soon as the others, and in particular Epaphroditus, who had been charged with her safe keeping, had become convinced that her state of mind was as she described it and so relaxed their strict surveillance, she prepared to die as painlessly as possible. First she gave a sealed paper to Epaphroditus himself to deliver, in which she begged Octavian to give orders for her to be buried beside Antony. She pretended that the letter concerned some other matter, and using this pretext to get the freedman out of the way, she set about her task. She put on her finest robes, seated herself with majestic grace, took in her hands all the emblems of royalty, and so died.

No one knows for certain by what means she perished, for the only marks that were found on her body were tiny pricks on the arm. Some say that she applied

A Would-Be Pharaoh Meets His End

Had Cleopatra and her Roman lover/ally Antony won the battle of Actium and established an empire encompassing the eastern half of the Roman realm, Antony may well have come to share Egypt's throne as coruler; and he and Cleopatra would have initiated a new dynasty of pharaohs. However, the lovers lost the battle and retreated to Alexandria. There, with the local population in tumult over the imminent approach of Octavian and his army, Antony heard a rumor that Cleopatra had killed herself. In despair he fell on his sword. Soon afterward, as recorded by the first-century A.D. Greek biographer Plutarch, Antony's slaves brought him, mortally wounded, to Cleopatra for a touching farewell.

When he understood that Cleopatra was still alive, Antony eagerly ordered his slaves to lift him up, and they carried him in their arms to the doors of the tomb. Even then Cleopatra would not allow the doors to be opened, but she showed herself at a window and let down cords and ropes to the ground. The slaves fastened Antony to these and the queen pulled him up with the help of her two waiting women, who were the only companions she had allowed to enter the monument with her. Those who were present say that there was never a more pitiable sight than the spectacle of Antony, covered with blood, struggling in his death agonies and stretching out to herself an asp, which had been brought to her in a water jar, or perhaps covered beneath some flowers. According to others she had smeared a pin with some poison whose composition rendered it harmless if the contact were external, but which, if even the smallest quantity entered the bloodstream, would quickly prove fatal, although also painless; according to this theory, she had previously worn the pin in her hair as usual, but

his hands towards Cleopatra as he swung helplessly in the air. The task was almost beyond a woman's strength, and it was only with great difficulty that Cleopatra, clinging with both hands to the rope and with the muscles of her face distorted by the strain, was able to haul him up, while those on the ground encouraged her with their cries and shared her agony. When she had got him up and laid him upon a bed, she tore her dress and spread it over him, beat and lacerated her breasts, and smeared her face with the blood from his wounds. She called him her lord and husband and emperor, and almost forgot her own misfortunes in her pity for his. Antony calmed her lamentations and called for a cup of wine, either because he was thirsty or because he hoped it might hasten his death. When he had drunk it, he urged her to think of her own safety, if she could do this without dishonour, and told her that of all Caesar's associates she would do best to put her trust in Proculeius. Last of all, he begged her not to grieve over this wretched change in his fortunes, but to count him happy for the glories he had won and to remember that he had attained the greatest fame and power of any man in the world, so that now it was no dishonour to die a Roman, conquered only by a Roman.

Plutarch, *Life of Antony*, in *Parallel Lives*, excerpted in *Makers of Rome: Nine Lives by Plutarch*, trans. Ian Scott-Kilvert. New York: Penguin Books, 1965, pp. 341–42.

now made a small scratch in her arm and caused the poison to enter the blood. In this or some similar way she had died, and her two waiting women with her. . . .

Octavian Learns of Cleopatra's Demise

When Octavian heard of Cleopatra's death, he was astounded, and not only came to see her body, but called in the aid of drugs. . . .

As for Octavian, when he found that it was impossible to revive Cleopatra, he felt both admiration and pity for her, but he was bitterly chagrined on his own account, as if all the glory of his victory had been taken away from him.

Antony and Cleopatra were the cause of many misfortunes to the Egyptians and many to the Romans. These were the circumstances in which they fought the war and met their deaths. They were both embalmed in the same manner and buried in the same tomb. The qualities of character which they possessed, and the fortunes which they experienced, may be described as follows. Antony had no superior in recognizing where his duty lay, and yet he committed many senseless acts. There were times when he excelled in courage, and yet he often failed through cowardice: he was capable equally of true greatness of spirit and of extreme baseness. He would plunder the property of others and squander his own. He showed compassion to many without cause, and punished even more without justice. Thus although he rose from most weak beginnings to a position of great power, and from the depths of poverty to the possession of great riches, yet he gained no profit from either situation. Instead, after hoping that he alone would rule the empire of the Romans, he took his own life.

Cleopatra was a woman of insatiable sexuality and insatiable avarice. She often displayed an estimable ambition, but equally often an overweening arrogance. It was by means of the power of love that she acquired the sovereignty of the Egyptians, and when she aspired to obtain dominion over the Romans in the same fashion, she failed in the attempt and lost her kingdom besides. Through her own unaided genius she captivated the two greatest Romans of her time, and because of the third, she destroyed herself.

Appendix of Documents

Document 1: An Early Pharaoh Shrouded in Myth

Very little for certain is known about the early pharaohs of the Old Kingdom. By the time that Greek and Roman writers began visiting and writing about Egypt in the late first millennium B.C., the pyramid builders and other early pharaohs and their deeds had become semi-mythical. When the Greek historian Herodotus visited Egypt in the fifth century B.C., the locals recalled, among others, King Rhampsinitus, who they claimed was the predecessor of Cheops (Khufu), who erected the Great Pyramid. They told the Greek how a cunning thief outwitted Rhampsinitus, a tale (translated here by Aubrey de Sélincourt) that is charming but likely a fable. As for Rhampsinitus, no pharaoh of that name ever ruled Egypt; however, he may be a mutilated memory of Sneferu, the sixth pharaoh of the Old Kingdom, builder of some of the country's earliest pyramids, and father of Khufu.

The next king after Proteus was Rhampsinitus, who is remembered by the entrance gates which he erected at the western end of the temple of Hephaestus, and by two statues which face them, each about thirty-eight feet high; the more northerly of the two is called by the Egyptians Summer; the more southerly, Winter. The former they treat with reverence and every ceremony of respect, but their behaviour towards the latter is quite the reverse.

Rhampsinitus possessed a vast fortune in silver, so great that no subsequent king came anywhere near it—let alone surpassed it. In order to keep the treasure safe, he proposed to have a stone building put up, with one of its walls forming a part of the outer wall of his palace. The builder he em-

174

ployed had designs upon the treasure and ingeniously contrived to construct the wall in such a way that one of the stone blocks of which it was composed could easily be removed by a couple of men—or even by one. When the new treasury was ready, the king's money was stored away in it; and after the lapse of some years the builder, then on his death-bed, called his two sons and told them how clever he had been, saying that he had planned the device of the movable stone entirely for their benefit, that they might live in affluence. Then he gave the precise measurements, and instructions for its removal, and told them that if only they kept the secret well, they would control the Royal Exchequer as long as they lived. So the father died and his sons lost no time in setting to work; they came by night to the palace, found the stone in the treasury wall, took it out easily enough and got away with a good haul of silver. The king, on his next visit to the treasury, was surprised to see that some of the vessels in which the money was stored were no longer full, but as the seals were unbroken and all the locks in perfect order, he was at a loss to find the culprit. When the same thing happened again, and yet again, and he found that each time he visited the chamber the level of the money in the jars had still further fallen (for the thieves persisted in their depredations), he ordered traps to be made and set near the money-jars. The thieves came as usual, and one of them made his way into the chamber; but, as soon as he approached the money-jar he was after, the trap got him. Realizing his plight, he at once called out to his brother to tell him what had happened, and begged him to come in as quickly as he could and cut off his head, lest the recognition of his dead body should involve both of them in ruin. The brother, seeing the sense of this request, acted upon it without delay; then, having fitted the stone back in its place, went home taking the severed head with him. Next morning the king visited his treasury, and what was his astonishment when he saw in the trap the headless body of the thief, and no sign of damage to the building, or any apparent means of entrance or exit! Much perplexed, he finally decided to have the thief's body hung up outside the wall, and a guard set with orders to arrest and bring before him anyone they might see thereabouts in tears, or showing signs of mourning. Now the young man's mother was deeply distressed by this treatment of her dead son's body, and begged the one who was still alive to do all he possibly could to think of some way of getting it back, and even threatened, if he refused to listen to her, to go to the king and denounce him as the thief. The young man made many excuses, but to no purpose; his mother continued to pester him, until at last he thought of a way out of the difficulty. He filled some skins with wine and loaded them on to donkeys, which he drove to the place where the soldiers were guarding his brother's corpse. Arrived there, he gave a pull on the necks of two or three of the skins, which undid the fastenings. The wine poured out, and he roared and banged his head, as if not knowing which donkey to deal with first, while the soldiers, seeing the wine streaming all over the road, seized their pots and ran to catch it, congratulating themselves on such a piece of luck. The young man swore at them in pretended rage, which the soldiers did their best to soothe, until finally he changed his tune, and, appearing to have recovered his temper, drove the donkeys out of the roadway and began to rearrange the wine-skins on their backs. Meanwhile, as he chatted with the soldiers, one of them cracked a joke at his expense and made him laugh, whereupon he made them a present of a wine-skin, and without more ado they all sat down to enjoy themselves, and urged their benefactor to join the party and share the drink. The young man let himself be persuaded, and soon, as cup succeeded cup and the soldiers treated him with increasing familiarity, he gave them another skin. Such a quantity of wine was too much for the guards; very drunk and drowsy, they stretched themselves out at full length and fell asleep on the spot. It was now well after dark, and the thief took down his brother's body and as an insult shaved the right cheek of each of the guards. Then he put the corpse on the donkeys' backs and returned home, having done successfully what his mother demanded.

The king was very angry when he learnt that the thief's body had been stolen, and determined at any cost to catch the man who had been clever enough to bring off such a coup. I find it hard to believe the priests' account of the means he employed to catch him—but here it is: he sent his own daughter to a brothel with orders to admit all comers, and to compel each applicant, before granting him her favours, to tell her what was the cleverest and wickedest thing that he had ever done; and if anyone told her the story of the thief, she was to get hold of him and not allow him to escape. The girl obeyed her father's orders, and the thief, when he came to know the reason for what she was doing, could not resist the temptation to go one better than the king in ingenuity. He cut the hand and arm from the body of a man who had just died, and, putting them under his cloak, went to visit the king's daughter in her brothel. When she asked him the question which she had asked all the others, he replied that his wickedest deed was to cut off his brother's head when he was caught in a trap in the king's treasury, and his cleverest was to make the soldiers drunk, so that he could take down his brother's body from the wall where it was hanging. The girl immediately clutched at him; but under cover of the darkness the thief pushed towards her the hand of the corpse, which she seized and held tight in the belief that it was his own. Then, leaving it in her grasp, he made his escape through the door.

The cleverness and audacity of this last exploit filled the king with astonishment and admiration; soon after the news of it reached him, he went to every town in Egypt with a promise to the thief, should he give himself up, not only of a free pardon but of a rich reward. The thief trusted him and presented himself, and Rhampsinitus signalized his admiration for the most intelligent of all mankind by giving him his daughter in marriage. The Egyptians, he said, were the cleverest nation in the world, but this fellow beat the lot.

Herodotus, *Histories*, trans. Aubrey de Sélincourt. New York: Penguin Books, 1972, pp. 174–77.

Document 2: A Pharaoh Uses Propaganda as a Tool

As the supreme leaders of the Egyptian army, New Kingdom pharaohs regularly bragged of their military deeds. This is part of a hymn inscribed on a marker stone on which the pharaoh Thutmose III is accompanied by a goddess who has supposedly helped ensure his recent victory. Such words and images were effective propaganda designed not only to glorify the king, but also to enhance the image of the army and military service.

I have worked a marvel for you;
I have given to you might and victory against all countries,
I have set your fame, even the fear of you in all lands.
Your terror [is known] as far as the four pillars of heaven;
I have magnified the dread of you in all bodies,
I have put the roaring of your majesty among the Nine Bows.
The chiefs of all countries are gathered in your grasp,
I myself have stretched out my two hands,
I have bound them for you.
I have bounded together the Nubian troglodytes by tens of
    thousands and thousands,
[And] the Northerners by hundreds of thousands as captives.
I have felled your enemies beneath your sandals,
You have smitten the hordes of rebels . . . as I commanded you.
The [peoples of the] earth in its length and breadth, Westerners
    and Easterners [alike], are subject to you,
You trample all countries, your heart glad.

Quoted in J.H. Breasted, ed. and trans., *Ancient Records of Egypt.* 5 vols. New York: Russell and Russell, 1962, vol. 2, p. 263.

Document 3: A Pharaoh Corresponds with a Foreign King

Among the most valuable artifacts ever discovered in Egypt are the so-called "Amarna letters," a cache of nearly four hundred inscribed tablets found in 1887 on the site of the city erected by the maverick pharaoh, Akhenaten. Most of the letters consist of diplomatic correspondence between Akhenaten or his father, Amenhotep III, and the rulers of other Near Eastern states. The three letters below constitute an exchange between Amenhotep and the king of Babylonia, Kadashman-Bel. In the first, the Egyptian answers the Babylonian's recent inquiry about the well-being of a princess he had earlier sent to become part of Amenhotep's harem; the pharaoh tells the king that there is no reason to suspect any harm has come to the girl. In the second letter, Kadashman-Bel proposes that Amenhotep send him an Egyptian princess to marry. And in the third, having received the girl, he thanks the pharaoh for the gesture by sending gifts. These letters reveal that Egypt's pharaohs engaged in vigorous diplomacy as well as warfare.

To Kadashman-Bel, King of Babylonia, My Brother—from Amenhotep III, the Great King, the King of Egypt, Your Brother.

I am well, may you be well; with your house, your wives, your sons, your chief men, your horses, your chariots, and your lands, may it be very well.

I am well; with my house, my wives, my sons, my chief men, my horses, my chariots, my people, it is very well, and with my lands very well.

Verily I have heard the communication which you have written me, namely: "You wish, indeed, my daughter to wife, although my sister, whom my father gave you, is there with you, and no one has seen her as yet, whether she is alive or whether she is dead." These are your words which you, in your letter, have written me.

But you have never sent a *kamiru* [eunuch] who knows your sister, who could have recognized her, and could have spoken with her. The people whom you sent, there is not among them one who stood near your father.

You write: "Even if you command my messengers and your wives to come together in open session in your presence, and even if you, Pharaoh, say to the messengers: 'Behold your mistress who stands before you,' nevertheless my messengers do not know whether she really is my sister who is with you."

Why do you not send a *kamiru* who could give a reliable account of the well-being of your sister, and why do you not command him to go in to see her house and her relation to the king?

You write: "Who knows whether she is the daughter of a beggar, she whom my messengers see?"

These are your words. If, however, your sister were dead, why should it be concealed from you?

To Amenhotep, King of Egypt, My Brother—from Kadashman-Bel, King of Babylonia, Your Brother.

May it be well with you, with your house, your wives, your land, your chariots, your horses, your chief men, may it be very well.

Now, my brother, when I wrote to you to marry your daughter you said you would not give her, in these words: "From of old a daughter of the king of Egypt has not been given to anyone."

Why is that? A king are you, and you can do according to your heart's wish. If you give her, who shall say anything against it?

When they told me your answer I wrote: "There are grown-up daughters and beautiful women. If there is any beautiful woman there, send her. Who shall say: 'She is not a king's daughter'? If, however, you do not send anyone at all, then you will have no regard for brotherhood and friendship."

That we might be nearer related to one another you wrote me of marriage; and I, for this very reason, for brotherhood and friendship, have written to you of marriage. Why did not my brother send me a wife? If you do not send one, then I, like you, will withhold from you a wife.

To Amenhotep, King of Egypt, My Brother—from Kadashman-Bel, King of Babylonia, Your Brother.

It is well with me; with you may it be well, with your house, your wives, your sons, your chief men, your soldiers, your chariots, and your land, may it be well.

May it be well with me, with my house, my wives, my sons, my chief men, my horses, my chariots, and my land, may it be very well indeed.

Verily all that I sent you are necessaries for your house, and, in truth, I have ready all that was in the presence of your messenger who brings your daughter.

Verily I have sent you a present: three couches made of *ucsû* wood and gold; five thrones made of *ucsû* wood and gold; a footstool of *ucsû* wood.

Quoted in Josephine Mayer and Tom Prideaux, eds., *Never to Die: The Egyptians in Their Own Words.* New York: Viking, 1938, pp. 149–52.

Document 4: A Pharaoh Issues an Edict to Protect His Subjects

The royal edict excerpted here is the best-preserved and most fulsome surviving Egyptian document of its kind. It was issued by the New Kingdom pharaoh Horemheb (reigned 1323–1295 B.C.) with the intention of preventing state officials from overcharging and otherwise abusing the people while collecting taxes; and it illustrates that at least some pharaohs, though absolute monarchs, were concerned with justice and the welfare of their subjects. Note that in addition to providing penalties for abusing the people, the pharaoh appoints both supreme and local judges to hear grievances, determine guilty parties, and hand out sentences.

His majesty took counsel with his heart how he might expel evil and suppress lying . . . and [deliver] the Egyptians from the oppressions which were among them. Behold, his majesty spent the whole time seeking the welfare of Egypt and searching out instances of oppression in the land. . . . He spoke as follows. . . .

Unlawfully Confiscating People's Goods

If the poor man made for himself a craft with its sail, in order to be able to serve the Pharaoh . . . and he was robbed of the craft . . . the poor man stood reft of his goods and stripped of his many labors. This is wrong, and the Pharaoh will suppress it by his excellent measures. If there be a poor man who pays the dues of the breweries and kitchens of the Pharaoh . . . and he be robbed of his goods and his craft, my majesty commands: that every officer who seizeth the dues and taketh the craft of any citizen of the army or of any person who is in the whole land, the law shall be executed against him, in that his nose shall be cut off. . . .

The Poorest of All Are Tax Exempt

Furthermore, my majesty commands that if any poor man be oppressed by robbery, his cargo be emptied by theft of them, and the poor man stand reft of his goods, no further exactions for dues shall be made from him when he has nothing. For it is not good, this report of very great injustice. My majesty commands that restitution be made to him. . . .

Royal Officials Seizing Slaves

When the officers of the Pharaoh's house of offerings have gone about tax-collecting in the towns . . . they have seized the slaves of the people, and kept them at work for 6 days or 7 days, without one's being able to depart from them afar, so that it was an excessive detention indeed. It shall be done likewise against them. . . .

Soldiers Stealing Animal Hides

The two divisions of troops which are in the field, one in the southern region, the other in the northern region, stole hides in the whole land, not passing a year, without applying the brand of the royal house to cattle which were not due to them, thereby increasing their number, and stealing that which was stamped from them. They went out from house to house, beating and plundering without leaving a hide for the people. . . .

Two Supreme Judges Appointed

I have sought two officials perfect in speech, excellent in good qualities, knowing how to judge the innermost heart, hearing the words of the palace, the laws of the judgment-hall. I have appointed them to judge the Two Lands [i.e., Egypt]. . . . I have given to each one his seat; I have set them in the two great cities of the South and the North; every land among them cometh to him without exception; I have put before them regulations in the daily register of the palace. I have directed them to the way of life, I lead them to the truth, I teach them, saying: "Do not associate with others of the people, do not receive the reward of another.". . . How, then, shall those like you judge others, while there is one among you committing a crime against justice. . . .

Creation of Local Courts of Justice

Behold, my majesty appointed the official staff of the divine fathers, the prophets of the temples, the officials of the court of this land and the priests of the gods who comprise the official staff out of desire that they shall judge the citizens of every city. My majesty is legislating for Egypt, to prosper the life of its inhabitants; when he appeared upon the throne of Re. Behold, the official staffs have been appointed in the whole land—all—to comprise the official staffs in the cities according to their rank. . . .

Conclusion

Hear ye these commands which my majesty has made for the first time governing the whole land, when my majesty remembered these cases of oppression which occur before this land.

Quoted in J.H. Breasted, ed. and trans., *Ancient Records of Egypt*. 5 vols. New York: Russell and Russell, 1962, vol. 3, pp. 25–33.

Document 5: Seti I Boasts of Taking Prisoners

Among the more militarily successful rulers of the New Kingdom was Seti I, father of the even more successful Ramesses II. Seti was the first known pharaoh to confront the Hittites in Syria-Palestine, and his victories were marked by an extensive series of relief sculptures and inscriptions at Karnak, near Thebes. In the following inscriptions, the pharaoh boasts about capturing enemy towns and taking many prisoners.

Good God, mighty in being, great in strength like Montu, residing in Thebes, youthful Bull, ready-horned, firmhearted, smiting myriads [vanquishing thousands]; mighty Lion, tramping the inaccessible ways in every country; the prowling southern Wolf, circling this land within an hour, smiting his enemies in every country, mighty warrior without his like, an archer skilful of hand, setting his fame like a

mountain of copper, furnishing their nostrils with his breath.
Retenu [Syria] comes to him bowing down . . . on its knees.
He establishes seed as he wishes in this wretched land . . .
their chiefs fall by his blade, becoming as that which is not.
His prowess is among them like fire, (when) he destroys
their towns.

Chiefs of the countries that knew not Egypt, whom [his]
majesty brought as living captives. They bring upon their
backs of all the choicest [goods] of their countries. . . .

The victor returns, when he has devastated the countries.
. . . The chiefs of the countries are bound [tied up] before
him. . . .

Great chiefs of Retenu the wretched, whom his majesty
carried off in his victories. . . . The chiefs of the countries,
they say in acclaiming his majesty, in magnifying his might:
"Hail to thee, O king of Egypt, Sun of the Nine Bows. Great
is thy fame, O lord of gods, (for) thou hast carried away all
the countries, thou bindest them beneath the two feet of thy
son Horus, Vivifier of the Two Lands."

Quoted in J.H. Breasted, ed. and trans., *Ancient Records of Egypt*. 5 vols. New York:
Russell and Russell, 1962, vol. 3, pp. 73–75.

Document 6: Ramesses III Defeats the Sea Peoples

*The last successful pharaoh of the New Kingdom, Ramesses III,
was most famous for his defeat of the so-called Sea Peoples (invaders from southeastern Europe) about 1176 B.C. in a large
naval battle fought in the Nile Delta. The incident was captured
for posterity in a stunning stone relief in Ramesses' mortuary temple at Medinat Habu (near Thebes). As a primary source, the relief must be studied in person or described to be appreciated; and
the following description is by scholar Manuel Robbins.*

The Sea Battle sculptural relief on the north wall of the temple is about 55 feet wide and . . . was originally augmented
with plaster and paint. Here, represented in a compressed
composition at which the Egyptians were very skilled was a
clash which occurred on the water somewhere near shore.
. . . On the right stands the pharaoh . . . gigantic in stature—

launching shafts at the enemy from his unerring bow. Stretching across the bottom of the illustration are Egyptian soldiers, marching off with Sea Peoples prisoners. On the left is the battle on the water. . . . Here there is a clash among ships. All ships are shown broadside, which enabled the master designer of the scene to avoid problems of perspective while still enabling him to maximize the number of ships and the number of men shown. . . . Ships are arranged in three rows, one above the other. In each row there are three ships. Three along the left and one on the lower right are manned by Egyptians, and the rest are those of the Sea Peoples. . . . Two of these Sea Peoples ships are manned by warriors who wear . . . feathered headgear . . . and two others by those in horned helmets. . . . Relying, perhaps, on their hand-to-hand combat superiority, the Sea Peoples came armed only with close-combat weapons—dirk [daggerlike] swords and a few lances—and that was a fatal mistake. The Egyptian forces, on the other hand, had not only close-combat weapons but stand-off weapons as well, their bows. With these they had reaped havoc on the Sea Peoples in their ships before they could close with the Egyptian [ships]. The scene shows a fierce mêlée of close combat. Egyptian boats have their oars out so that they are able to maneuver, but in the Sea Peoples boats, oars are shipped [pulled inside the vessels]. They are unable to maneuver. They have been caught by surprise it seems. From a crow's nest on an Egyptian ship, a slinger rains missiles down on the Sea Peoples. A grappling hook has been swung out from an Egyptian ship and lands on a Sea Peoples ship. The ship is hauled close and a Sea Peoples fighter is dispatched with a lance. Another Sea Peoples ship is dismasted, a third capsized. Sea Peoples are in disarray, drowned, dead. The water is filled with them. Those still living are fished out, to be sent to shore to join the line of captives.

Manuel Robbins, *The Collapse of the Bronze Age: The Story of Greece, Troy, Israel, Egypt, and the Peoples of the Sea*. San Jose, CA: Authors Choice Press, 2001, pp. 284–86.

Document 7: The Pharaoh Fights Like an Enraged Lion

Accompanying the relief sculptures depicting Ramesses III's defeat of the Sea Peoples (at Medinat Habu) are inscriptions. In this section of the ancient text, Ramesses is compared to "an enraged lion," an invincible hero beating back the invaders, whose boats capsize, sending them to watery graves.

Lo, the [peoples of the] northern countries [i.e., the homelands of the Sea Peoples], which are in their isles, are restless in their limbs; they infest the ways of the [Egyptian and other Near Eastern] harbor-mouths. Their nostrils and their hearts cease breathing breath, when his majesty goes forth like a storm-wind against them, fighting upon the strand like a warrior. . . . Terror of him penetrates into their limbs. Capsized and perishing in their places, their hearts are taken, their souls fly away, and their weapons are cast out upon the sea. His arrows pierce whomsoever he will among them, and he who is hit falls into the water. His majesty is like an enraged lion, tearing him that confronts him with his hands; fighting at close quarters on his right, valiant on his left, he has crushed every land beneath his feet.

Quoted in J.H. Breasted, ed. and trans., *Ancient Records of Egypt*. 5 vols. New York: Russell and Russell, 1962, vol. 4, pp. 44–45.

Document 8: A Female Pharaoh on Her Pleasure Barge

One of the most famous images of Cleopatra, last of the Egyptian pharaohs, to survive from antiquity was her grand entrance into Tarsus, in southern Asia Minor, in the late summer of 41 B.C. The Roman notable Mark Antony had summoned her to his headquarters there, and was quite unprepared for her boldness, theatricality, and considerable charms. Not long afterward they became lovers and allies, setting the stage for their war against his Roman rival, Octavian. According to Antony's ancient Greek biographer, Plutarch:

She came sailing up the river Cydnus in a barge with a stern of gold, its purple sails billowing in the wind, while her rowers caressed the water with oars of silver which dipped in time to the music of the flute, accompanied by pipes and lutes. Cleopatra herself reclined beneath a canopy of gold cloth, dressed as Venus [goddess of love], as we see her in paintings, while on either side to complete the picture stood boys costumed as Cupids, who cooled her with fans. Instead of a crew, her barge was lined with the most beautiful of her waiting-women attired as Nereids and Graces [minor goddesses], some at the rudders, others at the tackle of the sails, and all the while an indescribably rich perfume . . . was wafted from the vessel to the river-banks. Great multitudes [of local people] accompanied this royal progress, some of them following the queen on both sides of the river from its very mouth, while others hurried down from the city of Tarsus to gaze at the sight. . . . Gradually the crowds drifted away from the marketplace, where Antony awaited the queen enthroned on his tribunal, until at last he was left sitting quite alone and the word spread on every side that Venus had come to revel with Bacchus [or Dionysus, a reference to Antony's identification of himself with this popular fertility god] for the happiness of Asia. Antony then sent a message inviting Cleopatra to dine with him, but she thought it more appropriate that he should come to her, and so, as he wished to show his courtesy and good will, he accepted and went. He found the preparations made to receive him magnificent beyond words.

Plutarch, *Life of Antony*, in *Parallel Lives*, excerpted in *Makers of Rome: Nine Lives by Plutarch*, trans. Ian Scott-Kilvert. New York: Penguin Books, 1965, p. 293.

Document 9: Cleopatra's Tax Decree

Evidence for how efficiently Cleopatra administered Egypt on her own, during the years after Caesar's death, when she was allied with Mark Antony, is scarce. What little evidence does exist suggests that she was a caring, capable, and efficient ruler who managed the economy well and treated her people justly. During her reign, in glaring contrast to those of her Ptolemaic predecessors, there were no rebellions and tax collection proceeded normally. She improved and expanded agriculture, producing large surpluses of grain and other foodstuffs, thus eliminating food shortages and lowering food prices. One modest piece of proof of her wise administrative policies and concern for her people's welfare takes the form of a surviving decree, issued in her name, and also in the name of her son, Caesarion, on April 13, 41 B.C.:

Nobody should demand of them [the farmers] anything above the essential Royal Dues [basic taxes], [or] attempt to act wrongfully and to include them among those of whom rural and provincial dues, which are not their concern, are exacted [collected]. We, being extremely indignant [about overtaxation] and considering it well to issue a General and Universal Ordinance [nationwide regulation] regarding the whole matter, have decreed that all those from the City, who carry on agricultural work in the country, shall not be subjected, as others are, to demands for *stephanoi* and *epigraphai* [gifts and special taxes people were forced to give the government] such as may be made from time to time. . . . Nor shall any new tax be required of them. But when they have once paid the essential Dues, in kind [in the form of goods and services] or in cash, for cornland and for vineland . . . they shall not be molested for anything further, on any pretext whatever. Let it be done accordingly, and this [decree] put up in public, according to Law.

Quoted in Jack Lindsay, *Cleopatra*. London: Constable, 1970, pp. 127–28.

Chronology

B.C.
ca. 5500–3100
Years of Egypt's Predynastic Period, in which two or more kingdoms coexist and likely compete in the Nile Valley.

ca. 3150–3100
A powerful ruler named Menes (or Narmer) unites the kingdoms of Upper and Lower Egypt, creating the world's first true nation-state.

ca. 2700–2180
Years of the Old Kingdom, during which most of Egypt's pyramids are built, including the largest ones, at Giza, near modern Cairo.

2598–2566
Reign of the pharaoh Khufu (whom the Greeks called Cheops), who erects the largest of all the pyramids for his tomb.

2050–1650
Years of the Middle Kingdom, in which the Egyptians begin expanding their territory by conquest and their wealth through trade.

1650–1550
Years in which Egypt is occupied by the Hyksos, a warlike Near Eastern people who take over northern Egypt.

1550–1070
Years of the New Kingdom, in which a series of vigorous pharaohs create an Egyptian empire.

1479–1425
Reign of Thutmose III, greatest of Egypt's conqueror-kings, who rules the empire at its largest extent.

1352–1336
Reign of Amenhotep IV, who changes his name to Akhenaten in the process of launching a religious revolution in which he favors the face of the sun (the Aten) over the traditional Egyptian gods.

1336–1327
Reign of the young and fairly obscure pharaoh Tutankhamen, popularly known today as "King Tut."

1279–1213
Reign of Ramesses II, who fights the Hittites (who hail from what is now Turkey) in a great battle (the first in recorded history about which details are known) at Kadesh, in Syria.

1184–1153
Reign of Ramesses III, who defeats the Sea Peoples (invaders from the north) near the Nile Delta.

1069–747
Years of the Third Intermediate Period, in which the strong nation established during the New Kingdom becomes disunited and undergoes decline.

747–332
Years of the Late Period, during much of which Egypt comes under the rule of foreigners, including Assyrians, Persians, and Greeks. In 332 B.C., Greek conqueror Alexander the Great enters Egypt, liberating it from the Persians, but

at the same time introducing Greek culture and political dominance.

331

Alexander establishes Alexandria in the eastern Nile Delta. The city quickly becomes one of the greatest and most prosperous in the Mediterranean world, eventually second only to Rome.

323

Alexander dies. Soon afterward, one of his generals, Ptolemy, makes himself pharaoh of Egypt, beginning a new royal line, the Ptolemaic.

31

Cleopatra VII, last of the Ptolemies, and the last independent ruler of Egypt, is defeated by the Romans at Actium, in Greece. The following year, she commits suicide and Rome makes Egypt a province in its own empire.

A.D.
ca. 639–642

Arab armies seize control of Egypt from the Byzantine Empire, which had inherited the area when the western Roman Empire disintegrated in the prior century. The Arabs introduce the Arabic language and the religion of Islam.

1798

French conqueror Napoléon invades Egypt, bringing along over a hundred scholars to study the country's ancient monuments.

1799

Discovery of the Rosetta Stone, which proves to be the key to deciphering hieroglyphics, the picture language used by the ancient Egyptians.

1922
English archaeologist Howard Carter enters King Tut's tomb, which proves to be filled with golden artifacts, a find that creates a worldwide sensation.

1990s
Archaeologists begin unearthing the remains of the settlements that housed the workers who erected the great pyramids at Giza.

For Further Research

Ancient Sources in Translation

J.H. Breasted, ed. and trans., *Ancient Records of Egypt*. 5 vols. New York: Russell and Russell, 1962.

———, trans., *The Edwin Smith Surgical Papyrus*. Chicago: University of Chicago Press, 1930.

Dio Cassius, *Roman History*. Trans. Ian Scott-Kilvert. New York: Penguin Books, 1987.

Herodotus, *Histories*. Trans. Aubrey de Sélincourt. New York: Penguin Books, 1972.

The Holy Bible. Revised Standard Version. New York: Thomas Nelson and Sons, 1952.

S. Langdon and A.H. Gardiner, "The Treaty of Alliance Between Hattusilis, King of the Hittites, and the Pharaoh Rameses II of Egypt." Trans. A.H. Gardiner, *Journal of Egyptian Archaeology*, vol. 6, 1920.

Miriam Lichtheim, ed., *Ancient Egyptian Literature: A Book of Readings*. 2 vols. Berkeley: University of California Press, 1975–1976.

Daniel D. Luckenbill, ed., *Ancient Records of Assyria and Babylonia*. 2 vols. Chicago: University of Chicago Press, 1926. Reprint: New York: Greenwood Press, 1968.

Josephine Mayer and Tom Prideaux, eds., *Never to Die: The Egyptians in Their Own Words*. New York: Viking, 1938.

Plutarch, *Life of Antony*, in *Parallel Lives*, excerpted in *Makers of Rome: Nine Lives by Plutarch.* Trans. Ian Scott-Kilvert. New York: Penguin Books, 1965.

James B. Pritchard, ed., *Ancient Near Eastern Texts Relating to the Old Testament.* Princeton, NJ: Princeton University Press, 1969.

W.K. Simpson, ed., *The Literature of Ancient Egypt: An Anthology of Stories, Instructions, and Poetry.* New Haven, CT: Yale University Press, 1973.

Modern Sources

Ancient Egyptian Life and Culture

Cyril Aldred, *Egyptian Art.* London: Thames and Hudson, 1980.

Bob Brier, *Egyptian Mummies: Unraveling the Secrets of an Ancient Art.* New York: William Morrow, 1994.

Lionel Casson, *Ancient Egypt.* New York: Time-Life, 1965.

———, *Daily Life in Ancient Egypt.* New York: American Heritage, 1975.

Sergio Donadoni, ed., *The Egyptians.* Trans. Robert Bianchi et al. Chicago: University of Chicago Press, 1990.

Jill Kamil, *The Ancient Egyptians: Life in the Old Kingdom.* Cairo: American University in Cairo Press, 1996.

Barbara Mertz, *Red Land, Black Land: Daily Life in Ancient Egypt.* New York: Dodd, Mead, 1978.

Lynn Meskell, *Private Life in New Kingdom Egypt.* Princeton, NJ: Princeton University Press, 2002.

Don Nardo, *Egyptian Mythology.* Berkeley Heights, NJ: Enslow, 2000.

———, *Pyramids of Egypt.* New York: Franklin Watts, 2002.

———, *A Travel Guide to Ancient Alexandria.* San Diego: Lucent Books, 2003.

James F. Romano, *Daily Life of the Ancient Egyptians.* Pittsburgh: Carnegie Museum of Natural History, 1990.

H.W.F. Saggs, *Civilization Before Greece and Rome.* New Haven, CT: Yale University Press, 1989.

Byron E. Shafer, ed., *Religion in Ancient Egypt.* Ithaca, NY: Cornell University Press, 1991.

Ian Shaw and Paul Nicholson, *The Dictionary of Ancient Egypt.* New York: Harry N. Abrams, 1995.

David P. Silverman, ed., *Ancient Egypt.* New York: Oxford University Press, 1997.

Lewis Spence, *Ancient Egyptian Myths and Legends.* New York: Dover, 1990.

Miriam Stead, *Egyptian Life.* London: British Museum, 1986.

Desmond Stewart, *The Pyramids and the Sphinx.* New York: Newsweek Book Division, 1971.

Eugen Strouhal, *Life of the Ancient Egyptians.* Norman: University of Oklahoma Press, 1992.

Joyce A. Tyldesley, *Daughters of Isis: Women of Ancient Egypt.* New York: Penguin, 1994.

Battles, Weapons, and Warfare

J.H. Breasted, *The Battle of Kadesh: A Study in the Earliest Known Military Strategy.* Chicago: Oriental Institute, 1903.

Silvio Curto, *The Military Art of the Ancient Egyptians.* Turin, Italy: Fratelli Pozzo, 1971.

Robert Drews, *The End of the Bronze Age: Changes in Warfare and the Catastrophe ca. 1200 B.C.* Princeton, NJ: Princeton University Press, 1993.

R.O. Faulkner, "The Battle of Megiddo," *Journal of Egyptian Archaeology,* vol. 28, 1942.

Mark Healy, *Armies of the Pharaohs*. Oxford, UK: Osprey, 1992.

Kurt Raaflaub and Nathan Rosenstein, eds., *War and Society in the Ancient and Medieval Worlds*. Cambridge, MA: Harvard University Press, 1999.

Nancy K. Sanders, *The Sea Peoples: Warriors of the Ancient Mediterranean, 1250–1150 B.C.* London: Thames and Hudson, 1985.

Ian Shaw, *Egyptian Warfare and Weapons*. Buckinghamshire, UK: Shire, 1991.

Historical Overviews of Ancient Egypt

J.H. Breasted, *A History of Egypt from the Earliest Times to the Persian Conquest*. Originally published in 1937. Reprint: La Vergne, TN: Simon, 2001.

Charles Freeman, *Egypt, Greece, and Rome: Civilizations of the Ancient Mediterranean*. New York: Oxford University Press, 1996.

Michael Grant, *From Alexander to Cleopatra: The Hellenistic World*. New York: Charles Scribner's Sons, 1982.

Peter Green, *Alexander to Actium: The Historical Evolution of the Hellenistic Age*. Berkeley: University of California Press, 1990.

Nicolas Grimal, *A History of Ancient Egypt*. Trans. Ian Shaw. Oxford, UK: Blackwell, 1992.

Michael A. Hoffman, *Egypt Before the Pharaohs: The Prehistoric Foundations of Egyptian Civilization*. Austin: University of Texas Press, 1991.

Donald B. Redford, *Egypt, Canaan, and Israel in Ancient Times*. Princeton, NJ: Princeton University Press, 1992.

Manuel Robbins, *The Collapse of the Bronze Age: The Story of Greece, Troy, Israel, Egypt, and the Peoples of the Sea*. San Jose, CA: Authors Choice Press, 2001.

David M. Rohl, *Pharaohs and Kings: A Biblical Quest*. New York: Crown, 1995.

Ian Shaw, ed., *The Oxford History of Ancient Egypt*. Oxford, UK: Oxford University Press, 2000.

Chester G. Starr, *A History of the Ancient World*. New York: Oxford University Press, 1991.

Reigns and Achievements of Various Pharaohs

Cyril Aldred, *Akhenaten: King of Egypt*. New York: Thames and Hudson, 1991.

Bob Brier, *The Murder of Tutankhamen: A True Story*. New York: Putnam, 1999.

Peter A. Clayton, *Chronicle of the Pharaohs*. New York: Thames and Hudson, 1994.

Leonard Cottrell, *The Warrior Pharaohs*. New York: Putnam, 1969.

Aidan Dodson, *Monarchs of the Nile*. Cairo: American University in Cairo Press, 2000.

Joann Fletcher, *Chronicle of a Pharaoh: The Intimate Life of Amenhotep III*. New York: Oxford University Press, 2000.

Mark Healy, *The Warrior Pharaoh: Rameses II and the Battle of Qadesh*. Oxford, UK: Osprey, 1993.

T.G.H. James, *Tutankhamun*. New York: Friedman/Fairfax, 2000.

Jack Lindsay, *Cleopatra*. London: Constable, 1970.

Don Nardo, ed., *Cleopatra*. San Diego: Greenhaven Press, 2001.

Donald B. Redford, *Akhenaten, the Heretic King*. Princeton, NJ: Princeton University Press, 1984.

Joyce A. Tyldesley, *Ramesses: Egypt's Greatest Pharaoh*. New York: Penguin, 2001.

Index

About the Editor

Historian Don Nardo has written or edited numerous books about the ancient world, including *Life in Ancient Athens, The Age of Augustus, Greek and Roman Sport, Life of a Roman Soldier, Empires of Mesopotamia,* and Greenhaven Press's massive *Complete History of Ancient Greece* and *Encyclopedia of Greek and Roman Mythology.* Among his volumes on ancient Egypt are *Egyptian Mythology,* a survey of Egyptian weapons and warfare, and Lucent Books' five-volume Library of Ancient Egypt. Mr. Nardo lives with his wife, Christine, in Massachusetts.

J

932.0099 Rulers of ancient
RUL   Egypt.

$34.95

DATE			

5/05